ORGANIZE to EVANGELIZE

A Manual for Church Growth

Larry L. Lewis

Foreword by Adrian Rogers

VICTOR BOOKS

a division of SP Publications, Inc.

WHEATON. ILLINOIS 60187

Offices also in Fullerton, California • Whitby, Ontario, Canada • Amersham-on-the-Hill, Bucks, England

Recommended Dewey Decimal Classification: 254
Suggested Subject Heading: CHURCH ADMINISTRATION—MEMBERSHIP

Library of Congress Catalog Card Number: 80-50394
ISBN: 0-88207-219-6

VICTOR BOOKS
A division of SP Publications, Inc.
P.O. Box 1825 ● Wheaton, Illinois 60187

Contents

Foreword

Larry Lewis speaks to us from a background of varied experience and training making him eminently qualified to author a book on church growth. He has served as a successful pastor of churches of nearly every size and type, from a small rural pastorate during student days to the large metropolitan church he now pastors. Regardless of the size or location, all his churches have experienced outstanding growth.

Sometimes we weary of hearing people who have never "done it" themselves tell us how to do it. The ideas expounded in this manual have been used successfully and proven worthy in the practical laboratory of Dr. Lewis' own pastoral experience. His years of service as a minister of education in several churches and as director of religious education for one of our Southern Baptist State Conventions add to the richness of his experience.

Above all, Larry Lewis is a soul-winner! He challenges the pastor to make soul-winning the top priority in his ministry. Churches he has pastored have consistently led their association and state convention in baptisms! In this day of declining baptisms and blunted evangelistic thrust, we need a practical manual to help us "organize to evangelize." Dr. Lewis has given us just such a book. I recommend that every pastor have this book in his possession and within easy reach, to use as a guide as he seeks to lead his church to maximum outreach and growth.

Dr. Adrian Rogers, Pastor
Bellevue Baptist Church
Memphis, Tennessee

Preface

My life and ministry changed in one day. In October 1958, while sitting in a seminary classroom, I heard Dr. Joe Davis Heacock explain the time-honored Flake Formula. Though I had never before heard of Arthur Flake or his now famous formula for Sunday School growth, Dr. Heacock convinced me that here was a plan which would work.

I had just become pastor of a struggling, east Texas church. This tiny congregation, which a few years earlier had split from an existing church, had struggled along with little success, finally voting to disband. I agreed to come at no salary and attempt to revive the church.

We set about immediately to organize our church and Sunday School around the Flake Formula. Within one year our little congregation had enrolled 183 in Sunday School, was averaging 103 in attendance, and led the 52 churches of our association in baptisms! This laboratory situation had convinced me that the Flake Formula would work.

In 1960 I moved to Columbus, Ohio to become pastor of the Parsons Baptist Chapel, a new mission then meeting in an elementary school building located in a housing project. The total congregation numbered 16 people.

My first meeting with this group took place in a member's living room. After sharing the Flake Formula, and telling them I believed it would work in Ohio as well as in Texas, they—all 16 of them—called me unanimously as pastor. Immediately, we began applying the principles of growth to this new church and community.

Did the Flake Formula work in Ohio? Within five years our church had grown to more than 600 members with an average attendance of 400, making it the largest Southern Baptist congregation in the Columbus area. By now I was thoroughly

6

convinced that the principles of growth could and would work anywhere, if properly applied.

My next pastorate was the real test. Certainly, the principles had proved themselves in the Bible Belt of east Texas and even in a middle-class, working community in Ohio, but would they work in an upper-class, suburban community in the Northeast? Would they work in a city where 80 percent of the population was Catholic and Jewish, and Baptists totaled less than 2 percent? I soon had the chance to find out for myself when in 1966, I became pastor of the Delaware Valley Baptist Church in Willingboro, New Jersey, a suburb of Philadelphia. Our little congregation, averaging 80 in attendance and meeting in the basement of a house, was a strange phenomenon in this plush, suburban community of new homes and upper middle-class families. Most had never heard of Southern Baptists and certainly had no intention of worshiping with us in a dingy basement.

Believing that people are basically the same throughout the world, we again organized our work around the principles of growth. In my first month as pastor at Delaware Valley, I lectured on the Flake Formula every Wednesday evening. We appointed a committee to study the principles and recommend ways we could apply them in our church and community. The result was a "Sixty-Four Point Program of Progress," which simply stated, means sixty-four ways to apply the principles of growth.

Within five years, our church had become the largest Southern Baptist Church in the Northeast, averaging 400 in Sunday School and consistently leading our association in baptisms. We purchased land and built a lovely new building, but lack of space remained a problem. Classes and departments continued to meet in buses, school buildings, and the parsonage due to lack of space.

After serving three years as director of religious education for the Baptist Convention of Pennsylvania/South Jersey, I became pastor of the Tower Grove Baptist Church in St. Louis,

Missouri. Unlike my previous small congregations, Tower Grove had a membership of more than 3,000, the largest of any Southern Baptist church in the state. It had one of the finest church plants in the Midwest with a large auditorium, a five-story educational building and an activity building with gymnasium, roller-skating rink, restaurant, and bowling alley! However, like many downtown and midtown churches, this great church had suffered from years of decline. From 1962 to 1971 Sunday School enrollment had gone from a high of 4,437 down to 2,241, and attendance from 1,953 to 716. A transitional community had caused many members to flee to the suburbs, leaving only a few faithful members to carry on. Many felt that the only future for Tower Grove would be continual decline.

Would the principles of growth work here, in a dying church and community? Could the Flake Formula turn this church around and get it on the move again?

Members at Tower Grove believed it could and would. Years before, they had seen the principles enthusiastically applied and had watched the church become one of the fastest growing churches in the denomination. They remembered several years when Tower Grove had led the Convention in baptisms, and they had faith that it could happen again.

Immediately, we started to apply the principles at Tower Grove. We divided classes and formed new units. We took a census of our community and prepared prospect cards for every class and department. We began weekly visitation sessions. We started a training program for teachers, visitors, and soul-winners. Bus workers were enlisted, trained, and sent out into the "field, white unto harvest."

Once again, Tower Grove was on the move. For the past five years, Sunday School attendance has increased each year and is now averaging more than 1,200. Enrollment is more than 3,000. Once again, we are leading our state convention in baptisms and attendance. "To God be the glory, great things He has done."

How many of these successes were due to the Flake

8

Formula? The consistent applications of the Formula's principles of growth were the bases of our programs of work in each of these situations.

In the following chapters, each of the five principles of the Flake Formula (along with additional principles I propose) will be dealt with in detail. My earnest desire is to make this, as the title suggests, a practical, usable manual on church growth.

You should read this book with pad and pencil in hand. If an idea presented here seems valid, jot it down on your "Do Sheet." After completing the book, prayerfully go back over the list. Mark out those ideas that do not seem pertinent or workable. Make plans immediately, however, to implement ideas you feel will work in your church and community. Assign each idea to an appropriate person with a suggested target date for completion.

May God bless your efforts with a successful ministry and a fruitful outreach for souls.

*This book is dedicated to my wonderful wife
Betty Jo
who has been a tremendous blessing
in my life and ministry.*

1
What's Happening in Church Growth?

Some churches are growing today as never before in the history of Christendom. In spite of humanism, communism, secularism, and materialism, the greatest churches in history exist today.

Prior to 1973 no church had recorded more than 10,000 in Sunday School on a given Sunday. Since then, a number of churches have had that many in attendance and some are now consistently averaging more than 10,000 per week. First Baptist Church, Hammond, Indiana recorded an almost unbelievable single Sunday attendance of 101,000 in May 1967 (Elmer Towns, "The Big Get Bigger," *Christian Life,* October 1976, p. 36).

A church in Georgia grew from 250 to more than 1,000 in three years and has had as high as 1,800 on special days. A church in Alabama grew from 1,000 to nearly 2,000 in less than one year. A rural church in Tennessee increased from 23 to 230 within two years, while another rural church in the same state increased from 70 to 300 (William A. Powell, *Church Bus Evangelism,* Woodlawn Baptist Church, Decatur, Ga., pp. 18-19).

First Baptist Church, Houston, Texas grew from an average attendance of 500 to more than 2,000 in three years. At First

Baptist Church, Raytown, Missouri, Sunday School grew from 883 to 1,269, while across the state in the St. Louis area, First Baptist Church of Ferguson grew from 553 to more than 900.

Who has not heard of the First Baptist Church, Jacksonville, Florida with its phenomenal growth from 1,250 to more than 3,000 in five years? Perhaps their simple slogan, "Always more than the year before," should be the watchword for every church.

Dauphin Way, Mobile, Alabama is one of many midtown churches in a changing neighborhood that has found new life and growth after years of decline. Attendance decreased from 1,869 to less than 800 in 1966. However, recent years have seen unprecedented growth and this same church now averages more than 2,000 in attendance. Another downtown church experiencing tremendous growth after years of decline is Walnut Street, Louisville, Kentucky, going from a low of 950 in 1970 to more than 1,400 in 1973. The Curtis Baptist Church, Augusta, Georgia increased from 479 to 1,389.

What can be said of church growth in the downtown and midtown churches can be said also of suburban churches. North Phoenix, averaging only 400 members 10 years ago, is now averaging more than 2,000. College Heights Baptist Church, Elyria, Ohio, starting in 1966 with only the pastor's family as members, now averages more than 700.

Eastwood Baptist Church, Tulsa, Oklahoma is another example of phenomenal growth. Starting with 35 members in 1955, this church now averages more than 2,000 in attendance (Eugene Skelton, *Ten Fastest Growing Southern Baptist Sunday Schools,* Broadman Press).

On the Move
Today, even many small-town and country churches are on the move. Amite Baptist Church, Denham Springs, Louisiana, the largest country church in the denomination, grew from 345 to 550 in attendance in six years (Elmer Towns, *The Ten Largest*

Sunday Schools, Baker, p. 134). Memorial Baptist Church, Gettysburg, Pennsylvania has grown from 77 to more than 300 in attendance in five years. A rural church near Scottsboro, Tennessee, located at the fork of two dirt roads, jumped from 30 to 230 within two years (Powell, *Church Bus,* p. 15).

The church growth story goes on and on. These are only a few of hundreds of instances where churches are reaching more people than ever before. But the sad truth is that while many churches are growing as never before, many others are declining and dying. Growth is the exception rather than the rule. In 1977 Southern Baptists, one of the most evangelistic, growth-oriented denominations, reported losses in nearly every area of work. Sunday School enrollment dropped from 7,458,375 to 7,430,931, a drop of .4 percent. Baptisms showed the greatest decrease in 29 years, falling from 384,496 to 345,690, a decline of 10.1 percent. The average Southern Baptist church reported less than 10 people baptized during the year (Baptist Press Release, "SBC Membership Tops 13 Million," *Word and Way,* Missouri Baptist Convention, Jefferson City, Mo., February 23, 1978, p. 3).

Why does one church grow while another declines? Often in the same city and in the same community, one will grow by "leaps and bounds" while another church will fall back and slowly die.

Someone has said: "There's a reason for everything. Nothing happens by accident." If a church grows, there is a reason; it doesn't just happen. If a church is declining and dying, there is also a reason. The downward trend can be reversed. Such a church does not have to accept its fate as inevitable. It can get on the move again.

Vision

In his book *Churches and How They Grow,* Wendell M. Belew suggests that churches which grow must first intend to grow. Having surveyed more than 200 growing churches throughout America, he concludes: "The church and its leadership together developed a strategy for growth. They intended to grow" (Broadman Press, p. 140).

Many churches die simply because they do not expect to grow. They have no vision. They do not plan to grow because they have no intention of growing and no desire to grow.

In many ways it is easier for a church to die than to grow. Reaching people takes time, effort, and money, the three things many are most unwilling to give.

No church will grow until it desires to grow, plans to grow, and intends to grow. Pastor and people alike must be willing to pay the price in sweat, toil, and tears.

Many pastors will never lead a growing church because they are not willing to make the necessary sacrifice. The pastor of a growing church must be willing to spend many hours every week in visitation and soul-winning. No church will rise above the pastor's example. No church will be a soul-winning church if the pastor is not a soul-winner.

William A. Powell believes there are two essentials to a growing church: (1) vision on the part of the pastor and people, and (2) a willingness to make whatever sacrifice is necessary to make that vision a reality ("The Basic Laws of Church Growth," *Southern Baptist Journal,* April 1974, p. 8).

Do you have a vision for your church and people? Do you see it "big"? Can you see your church doubling in attendance this year? Can you see it doubling in 5 years, or 10, or 20? It will never happen until you see it happening in your own mind. The words of Proverbs 29:18 are never more appropriate than when applied to church growth, "Where there is no vision, the people perish."

Vision Plus Hard Work
As important as it is, vision is not enough to assure growth. Hard work is demanded of the growing church. Growth goals must be set and a strategy designed to reach those goals. Remember, nothing happens by accident.

If attendance generally averages no more than 50 percent of

enrollment, and enrollment averages about 10 per worker, it follows that 20 new workers must be enlisted and trained before average attendance increases by 100. If attendance and growth are directly related to visitation, then an effective visitation program must be designed and implemented.

If a church does tend to take on the shape of its buildings, then space must be provided for additional classes and departments. In brief the church that grows must desire to grow, expect to grow, and plan to grow.

Mack R. Douglas outlines his simple formula for a growing church as follows: (1) set a goal; (2) get a plan; (3) go to work. Then he adds a fourth important point in his formula for success: "Don't be discouraged by anything or anybody" (*How to Make a Habit of Succeeding,* Zondervan, pp. 41-43). Surely, great success will come to any pastor or church that diligently and prayerfully follows that simple formula.

2
Everything Depends on Leadership

Lee Roberson, pastor of the 40,000-member Highland Park Baptist Church, Chattanooga, Tennessee, is credited with first making the statement, "Everything rises or falls on leadership." Nearly every authority on church growth agrees that the primary ingredient in church growth is the pastor himself.

Wendell Belew states: "The [growing] church has a leadership which speaks with authority. . . . They have been able to speak with authority because they had confidence in the truths about which they spoke. There were no uncertain trumpets" (*Churches and How They Grow,* Broadman Press, p. 140).

Eugene Skelton echoes this sentiment. Having made an in-depth study of the fastest growing Southern Baptist churches, he states: "A factor in the growth of these churches, and a fairly constant one, is the personal leadership of the pastor himself. . . . The personal commitment of the pastor . . . is the dynamic of his life. It creates the fire of leadership which makes possible his challenge to the church" (*Ten Fastest Growing Southern Baptist Sunday Schools,* Broadman Press, p. 152).

Although many experts in the field of church growth differ as to the relative importance of various principles and methods, not a one of them denies the importance of leadership. Without exception, they acknowledge that the pastor is the one most important human factor in the growth of a church.

C. B. Hogue, director of evangelism for the Southern Baptist Convention, emphasizes the important role of the pastor: "The most influential voice in the life of the church comes from the pulpit. . . . As the acknowledged leader . . . the pastor can profoundly shape the ministry of his congregation. . . . If he stresses growth, growth occurs" (*I Want My Church to Grow,* Broadman Press, p. 66).

Elmer Towns, author of *The Ten Largest Sunday Schools* and *America's Fastest Growing Churches,* states: "Some pastors seem to have an 'extra power,' so that the masses are moved by their sermons; their requests are unquestionably obeyed by followers, people seem to empty their pocketbooks into the offering plate, and sinners almost run down the aisle at their invitation" (*America's Fastest Growing Churches,* Impact Books, p. 193). It is Towns' opinion that this kind of leadership can be learned.

This type of charismatic leadership may be typical of the huge, superchurch but is probably atypical of the average growing congregation. Not many pastors, even of growing churches, have people waiting anxiously to "empty their pocketbooks into the offering plate," or to run down the aisle at their invitation. Most pastors, however, are unquestionably men of great conviction and deep commitment. In fact, Eugene Skelton minimizes the importance of dynamic, charismatic leadership. "The quality of leadership that seems to mean the most is not so much a dynamic personality as it is a depth of commitment. The people of the church respond to the depth of the pastor's desire to reach people for Bible study and Christ" (*Fastest Growing Sunday Schools,* p. 152).

C. Peter Wagner, associate professor of church growth at Fuller Seminary, Pasadena, California boldly asserts: "In America, the primary catalytic factor for growth in a local church is the pastor. . . . There is is every growing, dynamic church a key person whom God is using to make it happen" (*Your Church Can Grow,* Regal Books, p. 55).

What are the attributes of the successful pastor? Why is one man able to distinguish himself with a fruitful ministry while another, perhaps equally as talented, fails? The following are some characteristics evident in the life and ministry of most, if not all, successful church leaders.

Vision

The pastor must be a man of vision. "Where there is no vision, the people perish" (Prov. 29:18). Unless the pastor and the people share a vision of great things and better days, the church will never realize progress and growth. Enthusiastic, positive leadership is essential.

No matter what his talents and abilities may be otherwise, a negative, defeatist pastor is sure to lead his church to defeat. Positive, excited leadership is more important than location, programs, facilities, techniques, or any other growth factor. The pastor should be a man willing and ready to tame lions with a bullwhip and charge hell with a water pistol.

Dedication

The pastor must be a man of proven spiritual depth and dedication. The "super promoter" and the "organizational man" may, by the sheer force of their personalities and organizational geniuses, attract large attendances but they will not build great churches.

The strength of a great church lies in the spiritual depth of its people. Again, no church will rise above its pastor. It should be obvious to all who know him that he sincerely loves the Lord and loves the Book. His compassionate "shepherd" heart should be evident. He should be an example of the rejoicing, victorious, Spirit-filled Christian.

Let the pastor not be ashamed to call his people to their knees for prayer. Let him not be ashamed to weep as he pleads for the cause of Christ and for the souls of men. One lady said,

"I would far rather hear my pastor preach with tears than with eloquence."

Delegation

The pastor must learn to delegate responsibilities and involve others in the church ministry and witness. Perhaps the most unsuccessful pastor is the one who tries to do everything himself. He may work long and tirelessly but achieve very little unless he learns the importance of enlisting, training, and motivating others to share his work.

Many pastors kill themselves trying to do the work of 10 people. Others get along with comparative ease because they've enlisted 10 people to help them do their work.

The church should not be hesitant to employ additional staff as needed. The best money any church will spend is that invested on effective "people reachers." Money spent on negative, unimaginative, ineffective staff is a drain on the church budget and may actually hinder progress. Money spent on profitable, effective staff members, however, is an investment that will soon return rich dividends, financial and otherwise.

The pastor must select his staff prayerfully and carefully, paying particular attention to the staff member's record of achievement in other places. He must supervise his staff carefully, being sure they understand their duties; he should also job check frequently to insure maximum results.

Beyond the staff the pastor must dedicate himself to the task of involving his people in meaningful service. A church member will be more faithful, will study his Bible more consistently, and will grow more in the Lord if he is involved. Most important of all, no church will meet its maximum growth potential until the people are involved in outreach. It is the responsibility of every church to harness the talent and energy of every member in some place of service.

The Sunday School and the bus ministry are the two greatest organizations for outreach in a church. The pastor should strongly support these programs and give dynamic leadership and promotion to them. Every week, he should carefully study the Sunday School report and think in terms of new teaching units that should be started.

Example

The pastor should set the example in service and witness. The ministry is no place for a lazy man. The pastor should be known as a man who gives much time to visitation and personal witnessing. He should make at least five visits every day a priority item on his schedule.

He should be present for and direct the visitation sessions, including the Saturday morning bus workers' visitation. Only when they know their pastor is a dedicated visitor and soul-winner will the members seek to emulate his example.

Interpersonal Relations

Many pastors simply do not know how to relate to people. An inflexible, bulldog attitude is offensive, and a placid, could-care-less attitude is disgusting and ineffective. Many pastors would profit much from a course on human relations or from reading and studying in the area of positive, constructive leadership.

The pastor has a great and demanding task. He should be quick to acknowledge his own inadequacy and his utter dependence upon God. He must approach his task with sincere humility, knowing that apart from Jesus he can do nothing (John 15:5), yet with the confidence of one resting in the promise of Phil. 4:13, "I can do all things through Christ, which strengtheneth me."

3
A Formula
for Growth

What is the best technique ever designed to reach people for Christ and develop them in the faith? Many believe the answer to that question can be found in two words: "Sunday School."

Dr. Gaines Dobbins, long-time dean of religious education at Southern Seminary, Louisville, Kentucky, states: "Where Bible teaching precedes, evangelism has its greatest fruitage; where Bible teaching follows, evangelism has its most permanent results" (A. V. Washburn, *Outreach for the Unreached,* Convention Press, p. 27).

J. N. Barnette, director of Southern Baptist Sunday School work during its time of greatest growth, enjoyed identifying himself as an evangelist who saw Sunday School as the best possible way of reaching people for Christ.

The great American churches cited in books by Eugene Skelton and Elmer Towns make Sunday School the primary means of reaching people and winning them to Christ. Towns quotes the pastor of one of America's largest churches: "Every Sunday morning when I get up, I am concerned whether it has snowed, rained, or we have beautiful weather. I get knots in my stomach worrying about how many we will have in Sunday School" (*The Ten Largest Sunday Schools,* Baker, p. 133). All pastors would do well to share this intense concern for their Sunday Schools.

What determines the success or failure in growth of a Sunday School? Is it location? The facility? The literature?

Many years ago Arthur Flake, then a traveling salesman for a clothing company, made a study of successful Sunday Schools and why they grew. He discovered that some were well located while others suffered from poor locations. While some boasted fine buildings, equally as many had inadequate facilities. While some were pastored by dynamic preachers with forceful personalities, just as many had ordinary pastors without unusual gifts of oratory or persuasion.

Flake discovered at least five factors apparent in every growing situation. He later outlined these "principles of growth" in a book (*Building a Standard Sunday School,* Convention Press, pp. 21-39). This simple formula was soon dubbed the "Flake Formula" and became the directive for Southern Baptist Sunday School work for more than 50 years. Later popularized by J. N. Barnette and other Sunday School leaders, this simple formula undergirded Southern Baptist growth as it became one of the fastest-growing denominations.

What then is this "magic formula" that has worked successfully for so many years? Simply stated, and greatly refined, the formula involves five principles that are surely characteristic, at least to some degree, of every growing church:

Discover the Prospects
A growing church must have a method and means of discovering who the prospects are and where they live. Not only must names and addresses be ascertained, but this information must be tabulated. Lists of prospects must be prepared and put into the hands of workers. This is an absolute must for a growing church.

Howard Halsell, an employee of the Baptist Sunday School Board, tells of going to a church to assist in an enlargement campaign.

"Where are your prospects?" Howard asked, expecting the pastor to produce some visitation cards or a list of potential church members. Instead, the pastor rose from his chair, walked to the window, lifted the blind, and sanctimoniously declared: "There are the prospects. As far as your eye can see—prospects, prospects."

"Yes," said Howard, "and that's where they're likely to stay, until you get their names on a card!"

Expand the Organization

Obviously, the more workers involved, the more work will be done, if they are workers and not shirkers. New classes are started and new departments formed in order to involve more and more people in the reaching-teaching task.

One thing should be clearly understood. Sunday School classes don't reach people. Sunday School departments don't reach people. Church buildings don't reach people. Church buses don't reach people.

What, then, does reach people? *People reach people!* Nothing else will do the job. Only people reach people. William A. Powell emphasizes this concept when he states: "People don't come to church—they have to be brought! People don't study the Bible—they have to be taught! People don't accept Jesus—they have to be won!" (*Church Bus Evangelism,* Woodlawn Baptist Church, Decatur, Ga., p. 79)

What, then, is the purpose of splitting a class, starting a new unit, beginning another department, launching another bus route? It is to get more people involved in the outreach task. God blesses work. The more work done, the greater the blessing.

Train the Workers

Perhaps Flake should have said: "Enlist, train, and motivate the workers." Each of these is a necessary function in the growing church.

You are today no less than what you trained to be yesterday.

You will be tomorrow no more than what you train to be today. It is imperative that the growing church have a thorough program of worker recruitment and worker training.

Many corporations spend 20 percent of their budgets on worker training while many churches budget nothing at all for this important task. The secular business world places more priority on training people for profit than the church does on training people for Bible teaching, visitation, and soul-winning.

The growing church must train its members. Poorly trained, unfaithful, incompetent workers will turn people away rather than reach them. The untrained worker may destroy a class or department rather than build it. More people will be lost through the back door than can be reached through the front door unless adequate worker training is provided.

Provide the Space

Someone has wisely observed, "You can't put two gallons of molasses in a gallon bucket, even if you pray about it." Certainly, a growing church must provide space for continued expansion. New classes and departments must have a place to meet, and space must be provided for new people reached by this expanded work force.

Providing additional space does not necessarily mean building more buildings. In fact, a building program may be the worst rather than the best solution. Certainly, it will be the most expensive, and may be divisive and unnecessary.

Why not try a dual worship service and/or a dual Sunday School? A large church in the Chicago area now has six separate Sunday Schools every Sunday, with an average attendance of 15,000. Other churches have used nearby buildings as a solution to the space dilemma.

A church in New Jersey tripled its attendance in three years using church buses, school buildings, and the homes of members to house Sunday School departments and classes. Two thirds of their attendees never entered the main church building, even for worship.

Dr. Charles McKay tells of a church in Arizona which had so many classes in the homes of members, they bought the Sunday School secretary a motor scooter to gather the records.

Go After the People

Arthur Flake, and all Sunday School leaders since, have emphasized the absolute necessity of visitation. Surely, if there is a first among equals, going after the people must be number one. Discovering the prospects, preparing prospect files, enlisting and training new workers, providing additional space—all is in vain unless workers "hit the streets" and "knock on doors." Ultimately, it is the personal contact that makes the difference.

Kenneth Dean, consultant for the Baptist Sunday School Board, quotes a bit of appropriate doggerel:

> Methods are many,
> Principles are few;
> Methods often change,
> But principles never do!

Many years have passed since Arthur Flake first outlined the principles of growth, but they remain equally as valid today. Methods must change with each new era, but the fundamental principles which undergird the growing church remain unchanged.

Did you hear of the Australian who got a new boomerang, then killed himself trying to throw the old one away? Do not be guilty of "killing yourself," by throwing away old approaches which have proved effective, and toying with new ideas which may or may not be productive.

4
The Lewis Addendum

Perhaps at least three additional principles should be added to the "Flake Five." They are equally as valid as the ones suggested by Arthur Flake.

The Principle of Superior Programming

The growing church must concentrate on making its entire program a quality, pleasing experience for all who attend. Bible study, worship, music, and preaching must be of superior quality if people are to continue to come.

Perhaps the reason many people don't go to church is simply because they have already been! No amount of visitation can compensate for a bad experience and a dissatisfied customer— or parishioner.

A service that does not begin on time, a department director who is not prepared, a choir singing music that does not communicate or inspire, a teacher who is not Spirit-filled, congregational singing that has no life or heart, a preacher with no unction—all of these spell disaster for the growing church.

Perhaps most important of all is spirit. Jack Hyles, pastor of First Baptist Church, Hammond, Indiana, which has the world's largest Sunday School, believes evangelism is an atmosphere rather than a program, a method, or a technique. It is the spirit of a people who say, "We love you! We need you! We want you!" It is the spirit of a congregation willing to make any sacrifice, pay any price, do anything necessary, and everything possible to reach people for Jesus.

People will put up with nearly anything but an unfriendly church. They may overlook, for a time at least, mediocre preaching and sorry teaching, but they'll never forgive an unfriendly church. "No one even spoke to me," has been the epitaph on many a dead church's tombstone.

Why shouldn't the church have "outside ushers" ready to welcome members and visitors alike the minute they drive into the parking lot? Outside ushers can help people from their cars, assist them to the building, and offer umbrellas on a rainy day.

Why not have someone standing at every door to greet the people, assisting those who need help to find their proper places? Someone should be at the door of every department to warmly welcome and to shake hands with all who come.

Shouldn't the pastor be present at the door of the sanctuary, not only after, but also before every service, greeting and shaking hands with all who attend?

If the church is a family, shouldn't members warmly meet and greet one another in Jesus' name, even in the sanctuary? Greeting one another and affirming one another is the finest kind of worship. "Inasmuch as you have done it unto one of the least of these My brethren, you have done it unto Me" (Matt. 25:40). True worship is celebration; it is *koinonia;* it is praise and rejoicing.

Apparently, some people would be happier worshiping in a funeral home than in a power-packed church that's on fire and alive! May God deliver us from dead, cold formalism, and set His church afire.

Dr. W.A. Criswell, pastor of the great 30,000-member First Baptist Church of Dallas, tells of a recent trip into another state. On Sunday evening he and his wife visited a lovely restaurant for dinner. As soon as they pulled into the parking lot, they were graciously met by a parking attendant. With a friendly greeting, he assisted them out of the car and into the restaurant. There they were met by a charming hostess who showed them to an appropriate table. Soon a friendly waitress greeted them and took their order. Frequently, she returned to inquire if all was well. As they left, the maitre d' greeted them warmly and asked if everything was all right.

Dr. Criswell and his wife then traveled to a local church. No one met them at the parking lot or even greeted them at the door. They found a seat and suffered through a dead, formal service. At the conclusion no one greeted them or wished them well. They found their way back to their car, unassisted.

Reflecting on both experiences, Dr. Criswell said, "Had they both offered an invitation, I would have joined the restaurant!" God forbid that the church of the living Lord would be less appealing than a place of commerce or business!

The Principle of Sane, Sensible Promotion
Especially in our day and age, the growing church must take advantage of the mass media. Good public relations, attractive advertisements, frequent well-prepared news releases, and radio and television spots and features can all be of tremendous value. The growing church should explore every means possible for taking its message beyond the walls of the church building and into the homes of the community.

Campaigns, contests, and special days can all be used to great benefit if properly planned and promoted. True, a strong church cannot be built on gimmicks and giveaways. However, even a cool cup of water given in Jesus' name has its reward (Matt. 10:42).

Good promotion is justified by the fact that many people hear of the church who would not otherwise know it exists, and some people come who would never otherwise enter the door. If so, that in itself is sufficient reward.

However, if people continue to come after their first or second visit, it will not be because of gimmicks and giveaways.

Rather, it will be because their visit proved a pleasing and profitable experience. A friendly welcome, a devoted teacher, a well-prepared program, and the obvious presence of the Holy Spirit make the difference.

The Prayer Principle   *excellent*
One additional principle must be mentioned because it undergirds and engulfs all the others. This is, of course, the principle of prayer. God's work must be just that—the work of God. We can be nothing more than instruments in His hand, tools in His service.

Jesus said, "My house shall be called the house of prayer" (Matt. 21:13). Prayer must not be a mere formality—simply a way to begin or close a meeting. Prayer should be and *must* be the very heart of all we attempt to do.

Take time to pray! The pastor should never be hesitant to call his people to their knees in prayer. Nor should the deacons be ashamed to come to the altar to kneel in prayer. Ask for prayer requests, let the congregation share their needs, and "carry each other's burdens" (Gal. 6:2). Let the deacons assist with the invitation, kneeling in prayer with those who respond. Let prayer meeting be a *prayer* meeting. Invite the people, led by the staff and deacons, to the altar for prayer. "If My people, which are called by My name, shall humble themselves, and pray, and seek My face, and turn from their wicked ways, then will I hear from heaven, and will forgive their sin, and will heal their land" (2 Chron. 7:14).

At every service of the First Baptist Church of Dallas, Texas, the entire congregation kneels in prayer. A special altar rail has been constructed for those who respond to the invitation, and kneelers have been installed at every pew. What a sight it is to see this entire congregation kneeling in prayer! May their "tribe be multiplied" throughout the land!

5
How to Discover Prospects

Discovering prospects may be the number-one task in any church's outreach for the unreached. There is no easy way. But the task must be done and done well if the church is to experience growth.

An up-to-date prospect file is imperative. Not only should there be a master file for the church's general visitation, but also a file of some sort for every class and department.

The prospect file should be cared for like a baby—changed when necessary, corrected if needed, and fed constantly. Also, like a baby, it should be loved and protected. Cards represent precious lives demanding concern and attention.

Perhaps one of the best prospect files is the pocket-packet developed by Eugene Skelton. (See Appendix.) This three-ring notebook binder contains a packet for each prospect. The prospect's name, address, age, and other pertinent information is typed on the packet, with the identical information on a prospect card which slips inside the pocket.

When an assignment is given, the card is removed and handed to the visitor. The pocket remains empty until the card is returned. A notation on the packet indicates the card's assignee, and a written report reveals the result of the visit. The pocket-packet can be ordered from the Baptist Sunday School Board, Nashville, Tennessee.

What are some means you can use to find the names and addresses of potential members for your church or Sunday School? Kenneth M. Dean lists 101 different ways for discovering prospects (*People Search Guide,* Convention Press, pp. 4-5). Probably, an imaginative, creative person can think of others as well. The following 10 methods are those most frequently and successfully used by many churches of various sizes and kinds.

The Community Census

Every successful pastor should learn the art and the importance of the simple "door-to-door" survey. In this mobile, transient society, the importance and potential of the survey is even more pronounced.

Many churches, especially in urban areas, should plan a complete community survey at least every four years. Perhaps the best approach is to survey one fourth of the community each year.

Who can and should conduct the survey? Ladies, youth groups, lay teams—all make excellent surveyors if properly trained. First Baptist Church, Jacksonville, Florida has more than 100 young people canvassing for several hours every Saturday (Homer G. Lindsay, Jr., "How We're Building a New Testament Church," *Southern Baptist Journal,* 1975, p. 32).

A church in New Jersey surveyed more than 7,000 homes one summer.

As in every area of church life, it is important for the pastor to set the example. He should not be reluctant to go with his people "house to house." Few sheep are likely to go anywhere the shepherd doesn't lead them.

Telephone Survey

The telephone survey is a modern approach to an old technique. Most cities produce a crisscross directory listing subscribers by street names and house numbers rather than alphabetically. Such a directory can be purchased (or leased) by the church and given to the telephone canvassers, assigning each one a particular street or section. As many as 20 calls can be made per hour. Of course information on those indicating interest is placed on prospect cards and printed in the appropriate file.

Action
The newest twist to the age-old survey is called "Action." This approach, developed by Andy Anderson, simply adds to the standard survey a deliberate effort to enroll those contacted in Sunday School.

Anderson believes that people should be enrolled anywhere, anytime they agree (*Where Action Is,* Broadman Press, pp. 76-89). Hundreds of churches have increased both enrollment and attendance, using "Action."

Newcomers
In his book *How to Have a Soul-Winning Church,* Gene Edwards says: "The newcomer list is about the most important single necessity to locating evangelistic prospects. It is just about indispensable. . . . Such a list is available in every town and city in America" (Gospel Publishing House, p. 113).

If it's not available through the Chamber of Commerce, try the utility and phone companies. If that doesn't work, try Welcome Wagon or a real estate agent. The company that publishes the city directory may offer a newcomer subscription service for a fee.

If all else fails, go to the county courthouse and get a listing of new owners. However you have to do it, get this list. It is important to the growing church. Three things should be done with the newcomer list:

• A letter of welcome to the community and to your church should be sent to every newcomer. This letter must be attractive and neat, printed rather than mimeographed.

• Someone (perhaps a homebound widow or retired person) should be assigned the task of phoning each newcomer with a personal word of welcome. Prospect cards should be filled out on any who indicate interest in your church.

• Visitation teams should visit those who indicate interest. Let the newcomers know you care and welcome them to your services.

Form Letters

Many have found form letters a tremendous way of discovering prospects. (See Appendix.) As already mentioned, a letter should be sent to every newcomer in your community. Also, a letter of congratulations should be sent to every newly married couple and every couple with a new baby. A letter of sympathy may be sent to anyone suffering the loss of a loved one.

A careful check of the newspaper will provide names and addresses of all such persons. Members of the congregation can be enlisted to assist in this meaningful ministry. Again, homebound members or retirees often are anxious to help.

Each letter should be printed or carefully mimeographed and personally signed. (Perhaps the letter to the bereaved should be typed personally.) You may wish to enclose a Gospel tract and/or a self-addressed, postage-paid reply card. (See Appendix.)

Ministries

One of the greatest ways of discovering prospects is by meeting needs. The ministering church will always have ripe and ready prospects.

A food pantry, a clothes closet, a job placement service, legal aid, a counseling service, a day care center, a Christian school —these services bring a parade of people to your door. These are people for whom Christ died.

Every ministry should be redemptive. As important as it may be, no ministry is complete until those reached are brought to Christ. No one is helped eternally until he is saved.

Is a prospect card made on every person reached through your various ministries? Do soul-winning teams follow up in an effort to enlist him in Sunday School and win him to Jesus?

Bus Ministry

One of the most effective means of discovering new prospects and increasing attendance is the bus ministry. Many churches have found this the best means they have ever employed in reaching people. If properly organized, bus workers devote several hours every week discovering prospects and enlisting new riders.

Prospect cards should be made for every unsaved and/or unchurched parent. Sunday School workers and visitation teams must follow up in an effort to enroll these parents in adult classes.

Visitors in Sunday School and Worship

No doubt the "hottest" prospect is the person who has already visited your services, providing his visit was a satisfying experience. Visitor cards should be placed in the hands of every visitor every week, both in Sunday School and worship. Information from the card should be transferred to a prospect card for immediate visitation. In fact, someone should "telephone visit" each visitor that very day.

The pastor himself should personally visit every adult visitor, if at all possible. Visits should be made also by lay teams and Sunday School workers. Don't let this "hot one" get away! Bombard him with love and concern. Your visits say, "We love you, we need you, we want you!"

Inside Survey

Another approach might be called the "inside survey." Would you dare to go through your present church roll and list as Sunday School prospects all members not now enrolled? Better yet, would you dare to simply enroll them in the proper class and department?

Also, list as prospects any unsaved and/or unchurched family members. The average church probably could increase its prospect files 50 percent by doing this simple survey.

An effective twist to the inside survey is the Sunday School witnessing plan developed by R. Othal Feather (*Outreach Evangelism through the Sunday School,* Convention Press, pp. 34-42). The heart of this plan is an analysis and assignment meeting.

Here Sunday School workers from every department go through their Sunday School rolls listing every unsaved or unchurched student enrolled (youth and adult) and every unchurched or unsaved parent. Each prospect is then assigned to some church member for visitation and witnessing.

Referrals

What insurance company or sales organization could exist without referrals? Perhaps the best prospect for any church is that person "somebody knows."

One church had a "Who Do" Campaign. Every member present was given a "Who Do" card which was filled out and turned in that very day. The card simply inquired," 'Who Do' you know who might be a prospect for our church?" Members gave the names, ages, and addresses of prospects.

Of course, there are many other methods for discovering prospects. You must decide what will work for your church and situation.

6
How to Begin Classes and Start New Units

Louis Entzminger states: "It is useless to give . . . prospects to teachers whose classes are already large enough. . . . It is useless to take this census and put all these new prospects in the hands of the present teaching staff. *It is the enlistment and bringing into the organization new life and new blood that determines the enlargement of the attendance*" (*How to Organize and Administer a Great Sunday School,* Manney Co., pp. 18-19).

J.N. Barnette, dynamic Southern Baptist Sunday School leader and author of the Sunday School "Laws of Growth," believes most Sunday Schools will seldom enroll more than 10 per worker. Barnette says:

Enrollment increases in proportion to workers at the ratio of ten to one. . . . For nearly a half century, Sunday School workers have known that a church over a period of several years will maintain a Sunday School enrollment of about ten people for each worker. A church by unusual efforts may attain more than this ratio for a time, but it is most difficult to maintain for a longer period than a few months a higher average than the ten-to-one ratio (*The Pull of the People,* Convention Press, pp. 35-36).

This ten-to-one ratio has been a touchstone in Southern

Baptist Sunday School life for many decades. Churches have continually sought to expand their organizations, believing that additional workers would result in a larger enrollment and greater attendance. In most cases this has proved to be true, but not always. Why not always?

Sunday Schools are built by workers not shirkers! It does absolutely no good to divide a class, begin a new unit, or start another department, if dedicated, faithful workers are not available or cannot be enlisted to staff these new units. A poor worker is worse than useless and will destroy a class rather than build one.

The principles of growth (Flake Formula) must be taken as a whole or they likely will not work at all. For example it does little good to observe the first and second principles ("discover the prospects" and "expand the organization") if one ignores the fifth principle ("go after the people").

At the same time, what good will result if you organize a visitation program (fourth principle) but there are no ripe, fresh prospects for teams to visit? (first principle)

One of those challenging the principles of growth is Elmer Towns, who made a careful study of large churches where a so-called "master teacher" approach is used with many enrolled in a single unit. Challenging the classic Southern Baptist laws of growth, he says: "One of the foundations of Sunday School laws has been, 'Enrollment increases in proportion to workers at the ratio of ten to one.' . . . However, most of the ten largest Sunday Schools do not reflect this rigid law" (*The Ten Largest Sunday Schools,* Baker, p. 135).

In the back of Towns' book is an interesting chart. Here he has compiled statistics relating to each of the 10 largest Sunday Schools cited in his study. One column lists total income, another the amount given to missions, the Sunday School enrollment, the average attendance, etc. When one calculates the total number enrolled in these 10 churches and divides that by the total number of workers, the dividend is 10.8, or approximately 10 to 1!

A casual walk through the church where a proper student-worker ratio is not maintained will generally reveal the inferiority of this approach. Masses of children herded into classes and ordered to sit still while somebody lectures them is hardly quality Bible teaching.

When to Start
When should a new unit be started? There are at least three answers to that question:

1. When better Bible teaching will result. Quality Bible teaching demands personal attention. The worker is not teaching a lesson, a quarterly, or even the Bible; she is teaching a student. She needs to know that student—his name and his needs. She should be able to visit his home frequently and understand his life situation.

"Hey you, in the yellow shirt," is a poor example of a loving, personal relationship.

Also, it is important for children's classes or departments to be closely graded by both sex and age. To put all children together in one department or class is to have first-graders competing with those almost ready for junior high. To have all preschoolers in one unit is to combine bed babies with those in kindergarten. What high school youth wants to be in the same room with someone in junior high?

Even though enrollment may be small, it is best to start another unit if better teaching will result.

2. When enrollment reaches saturation. Even Jesus, the world's greatest Teacher, limited His class to 12! He could have had thousands. Indeed, thousands did follow after Him but only 12 were enrolled in His own, personal class.

Generally speaking, a class with over 12 is too big. You should plan toward dividing this unit soon or it will grow very little and very slowly, if at all. New units grow faster and reach more people than old, stagnated groups. The growing church will organize to grow, not merely to take care of present needs.

3. When competent workers are available. Never start a new unit with carnal, unfaithful workers, hoping it will all work out somehow. Don't say, "We'll put them to work and maybe they'll become faithful." You're gambling with souls when you do.

How to Start

How, then, do you start a new unit? Three optional approaches can be taken when attempting to start a new class or department. In the words of the ancient lyric:

> Good, better, best,
> Never let it rest,
> Until the good is better,
> And the better is best!

The optional approaches are listed in that same order—good, better, best.

1. Create a "paper" class. A church in Texas had gone defunct. A new pastor had been employed to help revive the church. Only eight adults remained. Each of them was designated as teacher of a certain age group and given a list of prospects. Most of them had no one actually enrolled but only a list of prospects. Within one year, however, the church was alive and well, averaging more than 100 in Sunday School. It can be done!

Occasionally, a list of chronic absentees is given to a special worker with simple instructions: "Here's your room and there's your list of prospects. Go get 'em!"

2. Divide an existing class. A better way, most of the time, is to divide an existing unit, making certain there is a balance of faithful attenders and chronic absentees in each group. Thus, there is a nucleus of the faithful present each Sunday who become co-laborers with the teacher in building the new unit.

Isn't it amazing how some people would rather split the church than divide a class? Their theme song should be, "I am like a tree planted by the water—I shall not be moved!"

3. Regroup an existing department. The best way to start new units is to regroup an entire department or even an entire age division. In this way, five classes are started out of four, or eight out of six. A good strong nucleus remains in each unit, yet room for growth is achieved.

When thinking of ways to start new Bible-teaching units, the sky is the limit. The Bible-teaching program is that program of the church designed to teach the Bible anytime, anywhere to anybody.

Don't overlook the opportunity to start extension Bible classes in rest homes, jails, fire halls, hospitals, college dorms—anywhere people will listen. Why not have a corps of dedicated Bible teachers at work all week leading extension Bible classes while others open their homes for Bible study groups?

Can those attending extension Bible classes be counted in your weekly report? By all means. If church-elected teachers lead the studies, and authorized Bible study materials are used, the classes are a legitimate part of your church's Bible-teaching program and should be counted as such.

Suggested Enrollment

SUGGESTED ENROLLMENT CEILINGS FOR SUNDAY SCHOOL DEPARTMENTS

Younger Preschool (0-1 years old) 12

Middle Preschool (2-3 years old) 20

Older Preschool (4-5 years old) 25

Children (grades 1-6) 30

Younger Youth (grades 7-9) 50

Older Youth (grades 10-12) 60

Adults (18 years plus) 125

SUGGESTED ENROLLMENT CEILINGS FOR SUNDAY SCHOOL CLASSES

Children 10
Younger Youth 10
Older Youth 15
Adults 25

7
How to Enlist, Train, and Motivate Workers

In 1966 a "critical issues" questionnaire was sent to Southern Baptist leaders and pastors. They were asked to list what they believed to be the most critical issues facing Baptist people and churches. In an overwhelming response, these leaders agreed that the number-one critical issue in Baptist life is the need for effective workers (H. Joe Denney, and Jesse D. McElreach, *70 Onward, Church and Associational Phases,* Baptist Sunday School Board, p. 1).

Enlisting the Workers
How do you get the workers you need to staff an expanding organization and insure a growing church? There are at least three ways to enlist needed workers. Perhaps each way should be employed in every church. No one way will work by itself.

But if the church will diligently pursue the task, God will bless them and the needed workers can and will be enlisted. Remember the promise of the Apostle Paul in Philippians 4:19, "But my God shall supply all your need according to His riches in glory by Christ Jesus." Surely the need for workers falls within this promise.

1. Pray for workers. Jesus Himself gave the ultimate

solution to the worker problem when He said, "Ask the Lord of the harvest, therefore, to send out workers into His harvest field" (Matt. 9:38, NIV).

Just as important as praying for souls or for God to provide the money to meet the budget is the need to pray for workers. This is not a suggestion our Lord has made; rather, this is a command. Jesus commands us to pray for workers. Might this be the reason many churches complain of a worker shortage? "You have not, because you ask not" (James 4:2). "Ask, and it shall be given you" (Luke 11:9). "If you shall ask anything in My name, I will do it" (John 14:14).

Do you pray daily for God to supply your worker needs? Do you pray specifically for a particular need, naming the department, class, bus route, etc., asking God to fill that need? Do you ask God to reveal a particular person to you by name and then do you pray for Him to burden that person with that need?

How prone we are to complain and how reluctant we are to pray! May God convict His people for this terrible sin of unbelief. And may we turn our complaining into praise, our murmuring into heartfelt petition, and our skepticism into trusting faith to claim these mighty promises and pray for the workers God will provide.

2. Preach for workers. Long ago the Prophet Isaiah heard the clarion call, "Whom shall I send, and who will go for us?" (Isa. 6:8) The voice of God has continued through the ages calling out those who will labor for the Lord. He speaks through His men, "calling out the called." The pastor must not hesitate to preach for workers.

The Lord Jesus preached for workers. He reminded His disciples of the urgency of the hour when He said in John 9:4, "I must work the works of Him that sent Me, while it is day: the night cometh, when no man can work." To some fishermen He said, "Follow Me, and I will make you fishers of men" (Matt. 4:19). Surely, every true Christian yearns to be a faithful servant and an effective "soul-fisher."

Shouldn't the present-day prophets of God preach for workers? We give an invitation for souls to come to Christ, for people to join the church, for members to rededicate their lives, for young people to answer the call to missions. Shouldn't we also make a plea for workers?

Why not say in the invitation: "Is God calling someone here to be a Sunday School worker? Is God calling someone to be a bus captain?" (You don't want him serving if God hasn't called him.)

Many churches sponsor an annual Worker Commitment Service. As people enter the auditorium, a card is given each person on which he is to indicate a preferred place of service. (See Appendix.) The music and the message relate to the idea of service.

At the invitation time, everyone present is invited to come forward with the card, indicating his willingness to serve in the coming year. What a blessing these services have been! To see the altar filled with willing workers is a thrilling sight to behold.

A variation of this approach is a commitment service for specific workers, such as bus workers, Sunday School workers, and church training workers.

3. Personally enlist workers. Remember the Parable of the Husbandman in Matthew 20? What did he do about the worker problem? Did he murmur, complain, and gripe? No. Rather, he "went out" after workers. He went out the first hour of the day, then he went out again the third hour, and again the sixth hour, then again the ninth hour, and even until the eleventh hour.

What did he say to these potential workers when he found them? Notice his appropriate question, "Why have you been standing here all day long doing nothing?" (Matt. 20:6, NIV)

What a question that is for our day! Souls all around us are on their way to hell; sin is abounding on every hand; workers are needed in nearly every church. Why do so many stand idle, doing nothing?

Notice the answer they give: "Because no man hath hired us"

(Matt. 20:7). This is exactly the reason many potential workers are not being used today. This is why the talents and skills of many are going to waste. No one has personally sought to enlist these workers.

Wishing for workers will not get the job done. Someone has said, "If wishes were horses, we'd all ride!" You must care enough to go to that home, sit down with the potential worker, and lay a challenge on his heart.

How can you discover the workers needed for an expanding organization and an ever-growing Sunday School? Make a list. Prayerfully go through the church roll and list the name of every member who might be a potential worker.

How do you determine a potential worker? Ask two questions: Would this person be acceptable as a worker if he agreed to serve? Could this person (through training, etc.) be made acceptable if he agreed to serve?

If the answer to either question is "Yes," list him, pray for him and go get him! When going through your church roll, never ask, "Will this person serve?" That is not for you to decide. Don't put words in this person's mouth. Let him decide for himself.

Training the Workers

Having enlisted the needed workers, how do you train and motivate them for service? Many and varied are the ways. Each church must decide for itself the best approach to take. But you must decide on something.

For the growing church, training is not an option; it is an absolute imperative. Your church will become no more than you train your people to be. Here are some training approaches in the order of preference:

1. On-the-job training. No doubt, the very best training available is on-the-job. Assigning a potential worker as an assistant to an outstanding, in-service worker achieves the very best in training. This "learning by doing" is a basic principle in quality education, which provides not only the best in training but also an additional worker in service. Such learning by doing is often important to the growing church, which usually is stretching human resources to the limit.

2. Local church training program. The Southern Baptist Convention Sunday School Board has prepared excellent materials for a continuing training program for potential workers. The course can be modified and/or adapted to nearly any church.

Classes can meet Sunday mornings, Sunday evenings, and Wednesday evenings; or just Sunday nights; or Sunday and Wednesday nights; or whatever best fits your needs (William R. Cox, ed., *Ideas for Training Sunday School Leaders,* Sunday School Board, Southern Baptist Convention, pp. 32-47).

At the completion of the course, some churches have a commencement service with caps and gowns and award certificates to graduates. Why not? If God's work is the most important work in all the world, why shouldn't those who have been trained be recognized?

Another local church training event popular in many areas is the one-day Worker Improvement Clinic (WIC). A Saturday is set aside for training, and a faculty of outstanding workers is enlisted, providing training for workers in every age group. Five full hours of training can thus be provided in one day.

A preparation week should be set aside at the beginning of each new church year to train the workers. This should be an annual event, without exception, in every church calendar. Although this training week may include some general sessions for all the workers, the major portion of time should be given to age-graded training for those working with each group.

3. Denominational events. Southern Baptist Conference Centers at Ridgecrest, North Carolina and Glorietta, New Mexico are among the finest training centers in the world. Hundreds of churches charter a bus, contract a lodge, and take their workers to one of these centers annually. It's worth the cost. Do it!

Also, most state conventions operate a conference center and provide training for the churches. At great cost, associations provide a variety of conferences, clinics, workshops, seminars, and rallies. It is wise to take advantage of these valuable events.

Motivating Workers

How are workers, thus enlisted and trained, motivated for continuing and effective service? Here is a list of events that some have found helpful in motivating workers:

1. Worker appreciation banquet. At the end of each church year, the church should plan a Worker Appreciation Banquet featuring an inspiring speaker. A highlight of the banquet should be the presentation of awards for work well done. Give a trophy to the class and the department that enrolls the most new people.

Also, give a trophy for the class and department with the highest attendance. Shouldn't faithfulness in God's service be recognized? Shouldn't work well done be acknowledged?

A pastor once showed a friend the church's trophy case, proudly displayed in the church foyer, and filled with trophies of every kind—bowling trophies, volleyball trophies, softball trophies, basketball trophies.

"Trophies for everything," lamented the pastor, "except for anything that's really important."

The purpose of the church is not to teach people how to bowl or play ball. The purpose of the church is to reach people for Christ. You should acknowledge the job well done by workers aiming toward that goal.

2. Campaigns and contests. Every year most churches conduct a budget campaign. Financial goals are set for every class; visuals are displayed in every classroom.

At least once each year, many churches conduct a revival. Extensive plans are made, people are organized, meaningful events are planned, a visiting evangelistic team is engaged—all to support the revival.

Likewise, the church should plan, at least once each year, a great Sunday School enrollment and attendance campaign, setting goals for every class and preparing visuals for every classroom. These visual aids remind the workers and members alike of the campaign, and chart their progress (or lack of progress) toward reaching their goals.

Some churches have found that a friendly contest with a sister church (or churches) is a tremendous incentive for growth. The church enrolling the most new people and/or averaging the most in attendance is, of course, the winner.

A "pay-off picnic" or "winner's banquet" can be planned with the winning church members as guests of honor. An amplified telephone can be installed in each church sanctuary to broadcast the results each week.

Perhaps a beautiful trophy could be awarded to the winning church, and a "winner's certificate" to each participating church. Each church should be acknowledged a "winner" in that each grew more, reached more people, and averaged more in attendance than it would have otherwise.

3. Red-hot pulpit. A leading Baptist pastor once was asked, "How do you motivate your people to visit and be faithful?"

"Simple," he replied. "I make it miserable for them when they don't!"

Perhaps this rather negative approach does have some merit. The pastor is commanded in 2 Timothy 4:2 to "correct, rebuke, and encourage—with great patience and careful instruction" (NIV). Certainly, if a worker is not doing his job and doing it well, he should be taken to task.

The preferred approach, however, is that of our Lord when He saw Jerusalem as "sheep having no shepherd" and wept over His city. The pastor should not be ashamed to weep over his city; to be filled with compassion for his people; to cry out unto God for lost souls. The example of such a spirit will set the church afire.

Worker Commitment Card

YES — I REALLY CARE — YOU CAN COUNT ON ME!
Worker Commitment Card

As a personal commitment to our church Bible Teaching and outreach ministry, I will do my best to serve in the following way(s):

( ) Younger Pre-School Worker ( ) Single Adult Worker
    (Nursery — Age 3) ( ) Married Adult Worker
( ) Older Pre-School Worker ( ) Bus Ministry
    (Age 4—5) ( ) Anywhere I am needed
( ) Children's Worker ( ) Other _____
    (Grades 1—6) _____
( ) Youth Worker
    (Grades 7—12)

I would prefer to serve in ( ) Sunday School
( ) Church Training
I am already serving as _____
    Name: _____
    Address: _____ (Zip) _____
    Phone: _____

8
How to Provide Needed Space

The saying, "You can't put two gallons of molasses in a gallon bucket, even if you pray about it!" may be true of molasses, but it is not necessarily true of people and of church buildings. You can, for example, put 200 people in a 100-capacity church building—if you don't try to put them all in at the same time!

First Baptist Church, Hammond, Indiana accommodates an average attendance of 15,000 in Sunday School in a building intended for not more than 6,000. How do they do it? By having Sunday School all day long, beginning at 9:30 A.M. and continuing through Sunday afternoon. Also, they use a number of other buildings located apart from the main church plant.

A church in New Jersey averaged more than 300 in attendance while meeting in the basement of a home. The little sanctuary where they met for worship could hold only 80 people. How did they do it? By using buses, two nearby elementary schools, a fire hall, and the pastor's home as classrooms.

Yes, lack of space is an excuse, not a reason, for a church's failure to grow. Often a pastor or church member is heard to lament mournfully, "We can't grow until we build, and we can't build until we grow!" What a dilemma! Or is it simply an excuse for "doing nothing"? Is lack of space a legitimate complaint or a "scapegoat" for lethargy? Without exception, there are answers to the space dilemma if you really want to find them.

Use Available Space to the Maximum

Adequate space is expensive. It costs much to build and a great amount to maintain. Use the space you have to the maximum.

Four or five classes meeting in the same large open room will function better than just two classes meeting there. Two classes in the same room somehow disturb one another more than several do. Sight barriers can be achieved with curtains or portable screens or simply by having students face toward the wall rather than toward one another.

Why allow expensive, spacious assembly rooms to sit idle during Sunday School except for 15 minutes during a department time? Is it good stewardship of God's money to build, equip, and maintain an expensive room, and then use it only 15 minutes per week?

Dual Sunday Schools and worship services are more the rule than the exception in the growing church. In this day of accelerated church growth, it is not uncommon to hear of triple Sunday Schools.

Do a "space walk." With clipboard in hand, walk through your building during Sunday School and make note of unused areas. Are there unused hallways? Storage rooms that can be used? How about a class in a lounge area? You'll be amazed at the idle space just waiting to be used in teaching the Word of God.

Graded worship services are often the solution to a severe space problem in the sanctuary. While the pastor preaches to the adult congregation, perhaps an associate, a lay minister, or children's worker can conduct children's worship. Maybe several children's worship services should be conducted.

Someone may say, "I don't believe in children's worship." Let a growing church with an aggressive bus ministry unload a bus full of children, sending them into the orderly worship service, and this "someone" may suddenly believe!

Should children be expected to "endure" an adult worship service, forced to sit still for more than an hour while their little legs grow numb from dangling over the edge of an adult pew? Where else, in the whole of society, is a child expected to sit still and not move for more than an hour?

How much better for the child to enjoy a worship service designed especially for him! A service with children's songs, a special feature, comfortable, age-graded chairs, puppets, a Bible story, and a brief, easy-to-understand message can be just for him.

Beware of making the children's worship service merely an extension of Sunday School. The child, like the adult, needs a change of pace. The service should be a true worship experience, not merely another hour of Sunday School. It should be a simulation of adult worship, yet designed for the child. There should be an attractive altar area with chairs arranged in auditorium style. The Vacation Bible School joint worship service is a good model for children's worship.

Use Nearby Buildings

Many public buildings, and some private buildings stand ready to be used by churches and church groups. Many of the great churches in America reach fabulous numbers by using additional community buildings. In many cases buildings across the town or city are used for extension Bible classes or entire branch Sunday Schools.

Some have gone into ghetto areas and ethnic areas with branch schools which are, of course, counted in their regular attendance reports. Why not? Thank God that someone cares enough to do something in areas of our cities which churches too often have left.

Many others are able to expand their Sunday School

organizations and attendance by starting new classes and departments in nearby schools, lodge halls, and other facilities. As often as not, the growing church will have classes in funeral homes, barber shops, office buildings, and beauty parlors.

Use Buses, Cars, and Station Wagons
For many churches, an aggressive bus ministry has created a space problem. However, many others have found the buses to be a way out of the space dilemma. Why not use the buses to shuttle students to nearby rented buildings for Sunday School? Or use the buses themselves for classes and departments.

One church installed ceiling track and curtains in each bus, making class areas. They also removed the seats from some old, inoperative buses, making open-room children's departments.

Will these kinds of drastic means work? Only if the church has the outreach spirit. If the church is determined to pay any price and make any sacrifice necessary to reach people, nearly anything will work. But if the spirit is not there, don't try it.

A New Building
Building new, additional space may be the worst rather than the best way to solve the space problem. Buildings are expensive; the task of building may prove divisive, and it is always time-consuming on pastor, staff, and people. Often both pastor and people are detracted from building the church while building the church building.

However, if the church can afford a building project and not be so burdened financially they have little left for other matters, perhaps this is the best approach. Certainly, the attractive space made available in a new building is much to be desired. If you do build, do it right. It costs no more to build an attractive, well-planned, functional building than one which has been poorly designed.

W.A. Harrell, formerly with the Architectural Department of the Baptist Sunday School Board, liked to define an "ar-chee-tect" as a "preacher who draws his own plans." Few pastors know how to design a church building, but equally few don't like to try! The poor congregation left behind, as the ar-chee-tect hastens on to another field, has to suffer the consequences. Succeeding pastors will see to it that his name is remembered in infamy!

A tremendous service is made available to Southern Baptist congregations through the Architectural Department of the Baptist Sunday School Board in Nashville, Tennessee. At no cost to the church, architects, engineers, and building consultants stand ready to assist in a building project.

These people know every detail of the Southern Baptist program and how to design a functional building that will best meet the needs of the congregation. Most other denominations have a similar service. Use it! It is foolish not to do so.

Concentrate on educational space. It is your Sunday School that builds a growing church, not a huge, half-filled sanctuary. How foolish to build space you don't need and can't afford! The psychological effects of an empty auditorium are disastrous. It is far better to suffer the inconvenience of a sanctuary packed to overflowing than the frustration of an empty auditorium.

Yes, lack of space is an excuse, not a reason, for a church's failure to grow. There are ways out of the space dilemma.

9
How to Organize an Effective Visitation Program

Organized visitation is a must. If people are simply left to their own to visit at their convenience, little will be done.

Lee Roberson, the Chattanooga pastor mentioned in chapter 2, was asked to come to a large, but dying church for a workers' rally.

"Tell me about your visitation program," Dr. Roberson asked. "When do your people meet for visitation?"

"Oh," said the pastor, "we don't have a scheduled visitation program as such. We have prospect cards available here at the church, and the visitors come by at their convenience."

"Now for the $64-question," Dr. Roberson continued. "How many came by for a card last week?"

"Only four," replied the disheartened pastor.

A survey conducted by the Research and Statistics Department of the Baptist Sunday School Board indicates only 8.6 percent of Southern Baptist churches have any kind of organized, systematic witnessing program (H. Joe Denney and Jesse D. McElreach, *70 Onward, Church and Associational Phases,* Baptist Sunday School Board, p. 15).

Could this be the reason baptisms are down, Sunday School enrollments and attendance are decreasing and Southern

Baptists are reporting a decline in nearly every area? No wonder the average Southern Baptist church baptized only 10 persons per year, and more than 5,000 churches reported no baptisms at all.

A Systematic Program
Pastor, do you have a planned, systematic personal program of visitation and witnessing? How many visits do you plan to make every day? How many every week? What particular hours do you set aside each day and every week for visitation and soul-winning? (Robert G. Witty, *Church Visitation Theory and Practice,* Broadman Press, p. 33)

Every pastor should plan to make at least 30 personal visits every week. Perhaps as many as half of these will be pastoral visits—delinquent members, homebound, bereaved, hospital patients.

But at least half (15 or more) should be evangelistic, soul-winning visits to the unsaved and the unchurched. Any pastor who will do this consistently will surely be responsible for winning many to Christ every year.

At a recent state evangelistic conference, a speaker asked those present (mostly pastors) how many had spent at least one hour the previous week talking to someone about the Lord. Of this crowd of more than 500, only 13 raised their hands. Yet, probably every one of them would agree that witnessing and winning souls is the most important work any pastor or any Christian can do.

Work of the Church
In his book *A Quest for Vitality in Religion,* Findley B. Edge draws a distinction between "the work of the church" and "church work" (Broadman Press, p. 78). "Church work" is the humdrum routine of necessary, but often superficial, administrative tasks.

After all, someone has to meet with the flower committee, get the church bus inspected, mimeograph the church bulletin, and take Sunday's deposits to the bank. Why not the pastor? Isn't that what he's paid to do?

On the other hand, "the work of the church" is to do what Jesus would be doing if He were "in the flesh" in your community. "And Jesus went about all the cities and villages, teaching in their synagogues, and preaching the Gospel . . . and healing every sickness and every disease among the people" (Matt. 9:35). This, then, is what your church—and you, Pastor—should be doing.

Did you ever go to the bank and find the president running the mimeograph machine? It's not that he's too good to run the mimeo, or feels that it's beneath him. Rather, he's simply too busy; he's got far more important things to do. True, the mimeo has to be run, but let others do it. Let the pastor give himself to study, to prayer, and to witnessing.

Some will say, "Shepherds aren't supposed to produce sheep; sheep produce sheep. My job is to 'equip the saints,' then let them do it." True, but every shepherd should remember he is also a sheep.

What is expected of every Christian must be demanded of every pastor. Sheep will never go anywhere the shepherd doesn't lead them. Pastor, don't ever think your people are going to be soul-winners if you're not a soul-winner. Don't think your deacons and Sunday School workers are going to visit if they don't see you visiting regularly and often (Witty, *Church Visitation,* p. 33).

Did Jesus think witnessing was important? Did He Himself set the example? Notice Him with Nicodemus, the woman of Sychar, and the rich young ruler. Notice how carefully He instructed the Twelve, then the seventy, before He sent them out two-by-two. Notice how He required that they return with a report and how He carefully evaluated the results (Luke 10:1-20).

Apparently the Apostles put a high priority on visitation and witnessing. In Acts 2:46-47, Luke said that the Christians continued "daily with one accord in the temple . . . breaking bread from house to house . . . praising God, and having favor with all the people." Luke added, "They . . . went every where preaching" (Acts 8:4) and soon had "filled Jerusalem" with their doctrine (Acts 5:28), and had "turned the world upside down" (Acts 17:6).

The Apostle Paul reminded the elders from Ephesus, "You know how I lived the whole time I was with you. . . . You know that I have not hesitated to preach anything that would be helpful to you but have taught you publicly and from house to house" (Acts 20:18, 20, NIV). The spirit of this great apostle is revealed in Acts 20:31: "I never stopped warning each of you night and day with tears" (NIV). For this reason alone, he could boldly acclaim, "I am innocent of the blood of all men" (Acts 20:26). Thank God for that kind of witness and that kind of witnessing!

Types of Visits
C.S. Lovett categorizes three types of visitation approaches in *Visitation Made Easy,* Personal Christianity, pp. 3-7.

1. The self-centered visit. The self-centered visit is the initial contact which seeks to win the person's friendship and confidence. Before you can win someone to Jesus, you must first win him to yourself. He must like you, believe in you, and know you are sincere.

"Howdy, stranger; are you saved?" is not an approach that wins many people to Christ. An expression of genuine concern for the person is a prerequisite to a successful witness.

2. The church-centered visit. The church-centered visit is primarily an effort to win people to the church or the church program. It is the Sunday School teacher inviting a prospect to her class. It is the deacon trying to "pack his pew" or the pastor inviting newcomers to the services. It may be a concerned neighbor inviting friends to church, or a bus captain seeking to fill his bus.

Much can and should be said in support of this approach. "Enlistment Evangelism" has been and probably will continue to be the most popular and fruitful means of reaching people for Christ and for meaningful church membership. Some have estimated that more than 80 percent of those saved and baptized in Baptist churches are reached through the Sunday School.

When a spiritually lost person, regardless of age, is persuaded to come to church, a great victory has been won already. If the Bible is faithfully taught and preached, it will undoubtedly make an impact. "My Word . . . shall not return unto Me void" (Isa. 55:11).

Use any means necessary, but get these unsaved people under the sound of the Gospel. Use goals, campaigns, contests, special days, and giveaways, but get them to church.

3. The Christ-centered visit. Although much good can result from the self-centered and church-centered visits, these are not the highest levels or finest types of visitations. Perfecting the art of the "Christ-centered" visit should be the goal of every Christian.

When the disciples returned, after having been sent out two-by-two, they happily exclaimed: "Lord, even the demons submit to us in Your name (Luke 10:17, NIV). They did not say "in the name of the church" or "in the name of the Sunday School class." The devils were subject to them "in Jesus' name."

Oh, what power there is in the name of Jesus! "In the name of Jesus Christ of Nazareth," said Peter, "rise up and walk" (Acts 3:6). "If you shall ask anything in My name, I will do it" (John 14:14). The Apostle Paul tells of a day when every knee shall bow at the name of Jesus (Phil. 2:10-11).

When you visit, talk about Jesus. Tell people of His love for them. Tell them that, even though they are lost and undone, Christ died for them and wants to save them from their sins. Show them, in the Bible, how they can receive Christ personally. Invite them to pray, asking Jesus to come into their hearts and forgive their sins. Offer to lead them in a simple "sinner's prayer."

Bill Bright of Campus Crusade has coined this simple definition of successful witnessing: "Successful witnessing is sharing Christ in the power of the Spirit and leaving the results to God."

Yes, if you've shared Jesus, you have been a successful witness, whether or not the person visited has been saved. Go your way rejoicing and simply leave the rest to God.

Scheduled Visitation

People left on their own to visit at their convenience will seldom visit at all. For a church's visitation program to be successful, it must be organized and scheduled.

This is not to say "lifestyle evangelism" (witnessing anywhere, anytime, to anybody) is not a valid concept. Certainly it is. Surely, Spirit-filled Christians will want to make an impact for Christ always and everywhere.

However, in order for ripe prospects to be contacted, visitors followed up on, newcomers invited to the services, unsaved Sunday School members reached for Christ, and church growth experienced, there must be an organized, systematic visitation program. Haphazard, catch-what-may approaches will not get the job done.

Here are some approaches used successfully by many churches. No church will want to use all of them, but every church should use some of them.

1. Ladies' visitation. Why not have a morning or afternoon each week when the ladies are urged to visit? Be sure to provide child care for the babies and children. Hire a sitter. It may be the best money you've ever spent. Possibly, you will want to plan refreshments or even a weekly luncheon for this group of faithful visitors.

2. Recreation visitation. Why not have an evening each week for youth visitation? Or perhaps Saturday morning might work better. Make the assignments, let the young people visit for an hour or so, then return to the church, with those visited, for directed recreation.

3. General visitation. Men and women should attend a general visitation session one night each week. Be sure to have up-to-date, ripe-prospect cards ready for assignment.

Again, it is important to provide child care for babies and children. Be sure to have visitors return to the church for a report time and refreshments.

4. Bus workers' visitation. Most churches experiencing real success in the bus ministry require all bus workers to visit at least four hours every week (William A. Powell, *Church Bus Evangelism,* Woodlawn Baptist Church, Decatur, Ga., pp. 191-193). They visit everybody enrolled every week, plus spend some time enlisting new riders. Is it any wonder bus ministries have doubled and even tripled attendance in many churches?

Bus ministry visitation is usually conducted Saturdays from 10:00 A.M. until 2:00 P.M. All bus workers, especially captains and co-captains, should be required to visit.

5. Sunday School visitation. Every outreach leader in youth and adult classes should be given three to five minutes every Sunday morning to make visitation assignments and receive reports from the previous Sunday. Make your Sunday School a "reaching" as well as a "teaching" organization.

6. Sunday afternoon "blitz." Periodically, perhaps the Sunday before every revival campaign, have a "visitation blitz." Provide a light lunch for the people in the church fellowship hall. While they are eating, give some simple instructions and make assignments. They can turn in reports Sunday evening. Be sure to provide child care. This approach also works well for a survey effort or "Action."

7. Zoned visitation. In large metropolitan areas, some churches have successfully used the "zoned visitation" idea. Here the city is divided into several zones with a host home in each zone.

On visitation night members who live in that area go to the host home for assignments and return there for reports. A staff member, or other designated person, meets with the group, makes assignments, and presides over the report time.

First Baptist Church of Houston, Texas has used this plan successfully. They divided the city into already established postal zones, with the zip code on the prospect card determining the assignment for visitation.

8. Reproductive evangelism. Probably one of the best approaches for witness training and involvement is the reproductive evangelism plan. This program is outlined in detail by D. James Kennedy in his book, *Evangelism Explosion* (Tyndale House, pp. 1-21). Many others have modified and adapted the plan to their particular situations. Literally thousands of effective soul-winners have been enlisted and trained by this approach.

The plan consists of 13 weeks of training coupled with actual, directed field experience. At the completion of the training period, the trainee becomes a trainer in the reproductive evangelism program.

For the next term, and thereafter, each trainer seeks to enlist at least one trainee. He sits with him during the 45-minute class session, then takes him out visiting for one-and-a-half hours. The trainee observes the trainer as he witnesses personally to the unsaved prospect, assisting as silent partner and prayer warrior.

Reproductive evangelism sessions can be held in the mornings or afternoons for ladies, in the evenings for men, or on Saturdays or even Sundays. Hundreds of churches have come alive and found unparalleled church growth as a result of reproductive evangelism programs.

Of course, there are many approaches to visitation equally as effective: Deacon visitation, Training Union visitation, Fishermen's Clubs for men, and many others. How sad, then, that so few churches have any organized visitation.

A pastor was visiting a fellow pastor at his church on a Thursday evening. As usual only a faithful few were present for the Thursday evening visitation session.

"Isn't this terrible?" the visiting pastor said. "A big church like yours, and so few present for visitation. That's why we don't have visitation at all in my church. Hardly anybody will come."

"Well," said his pastor friend, "poor as it is, I like the way we do it better than the way you don't do it!"

The truth is, only a few out for visitation will do more good than many out for nearly anything else going on. Someone has said: "The mob is a glob of slob!" Don't wait for the mob to go visiting. It's the Master's Minority that gets the job done!

10
Giveaways, Gimmicks, and Goldfish

A pastor was lamenting the sorry and dreadful results of a recent attendance promotion. His church had agreed to give a goldfish in a plastic bag to any child who came on a particular Sunday.

To his dismay, when the workers arrived Sunday morning to bag the fish, they discovered many of the fish had flopped out of the wading pool and were lying dead all over the floor. Furthermore, they had great difficulty getting the rest of them bagged and into the hands of the eager children.

On the way home, most of the bags split, soaking the laps of the children, and washing the goldfish to their doom. Frantic mothers called the church office, while disgusted bus workers swept out the dead fish.

"When you come right down to it," observed the pastor, "the Word of God effectively taught and preached is far more to be desired than goldfish in a plastic bag!"

So it is indeed. However, does this mean there is no place for sane and sensible promotion? Certainly not. But it is imperative that one realizes the limitations. A great church cannot be built on gimmicks and goldfish. However, neither do unsaved, unregenerate people respond to noble, spiritual appeals.

Evangelist Angel Martinez was first persuaded to come to church by the offer of an ice cream cone. He later became a Christian, won his entire family to Christ, and since has been used by God to win thousands. Thank God for an ice cream cone given in the name of Jesus.

In church growth no one is quite so naive as the one who says, "It won't work." God can, if He wills, use anything to His glory. However, equally foolish is the person who insists on continuing the use of methods and techniques that produce no results. "The proof is in the pudding." If your methods and techniques work, use them.

Use Methods That Work

Peter Wagner, church growth expert, Fuller Seminary, Pasadena, California says: "We teach men to be ruthless in regard to methods. If it doesn't work to the glory of God and the extension of Christ's church, throw it away and get something else that does. As to methods, we are fiercely pragmatic!" (*The Growing Church*, Fuller Evangelistic Association, Cassette tape 2, Side 1) Wagner calls this "consecrated pragmatism."

In his book *Your Church Can Grow* (Regal Books, pp. 136-137), Wagner pleads the cause for pragmatism and seeks to answer the question, "Does the end justify the means?"

We are unashamedly recommending a fiercely pragmatic approach to evangelism. It is a common mistake to associate pragmatism with a lack of spirituality. Some are rightly afraid that pragmatism can degenerate to the point that ungodly methods are used and this is not at all what church growth people advocate. The Bible does not allow us to sin that grace may abound or to use means that God has prohibited in order to accomplish ends that He has recommended.

But, with this proviso, we ought to see clearly that the end does justify the means. What else possibly could justify the means? If the method I am using accomplishes the goal I am aiming at, it is for that reason a good method. If, on the other hand, my method is not accomplishing the goal, how can I be justified in continuing to use it?

I fear that many have fallen into the trap of developing such outstanding programs with such well-oiled machinery, involving such substantial investments of time and money, that the program itself has become the end. . . .

A biblical proverb addresses this problem directly: "It is pleasant to see plans develop. That is why fools refuse to give them up, even when they are wrong" (Prov. 13:19, LB).

Seek earnestly the Spirit's guidance in developing outreach programs and plans. Boldly evaluate the results, readily discarding that which proves ineffective and using only that which reaps results. Pay any price, make any sacrifice, do anything necessary, and everything possible to reach people for Christ and His church.

Promotional Ideas
Consider some promotional ideas which may or may not prove of value.

1. News releases. The wise pastor has a loaded camera in his office at all times. A top quality Polaroid camera that can develop a picture instantly is best. When something news-worthy happens, get a picture, write a release, and take them to your local paper.

Use the news! A good news release, with a picture, is far better than any paid advertisement. The aggressive, evangelistic church should seek to have a news release, with picture, in the newspaper at least once each month.

"A picture is worth a thousand words." But let it be an action picture, not posed. Take profiles and frontals. Nobody wants to look at the back of somebody's head.

The release should be written in newspaper style, answering the questions: *who, what, where, when,* and *why* in the opening paragraph. Make the release brief and to the point—brief enough to be interesting, but broad enough to cover the whole story.

2. Advertisements. An attractive advertisement in the local paper should be a matter of course for the growing church. How big should the ad be? A simple rule might be: "A little bigger than anybody else's."

3. Campaigns. The growing church should plan for one or two enlargement and attendance campaigns every year. The primary emphasis should be on reaching and enrolling new people, balanced by an emphasis on average attendance. Banners promoting the campaign and visuals publicizing the goals are helpful.

A visual should be prepared for every classroom, publicizing the new member goals and the attendance goals for each unit. Also, the visual should chart the progress of that class toward reaching its goals.

Arthur Davenport Associates of Oklahoma City, Oklahoma has excellent prepared materials for many such campaigns. However, most of the Davenport campaigns emphasize attendance rather than enrolling new members and are restricted to four or five weeks rather than a longer period.

4. Contests. Many churches have used contests to excite action and outreach. Contests can be between departments within an age division, between classes within a department, or even between sister churches.

The three largest Southern Baptist churches in Missouri recently entered a contest to see which church could average the highest attendance and enroll the most new members. The campaign continued for eight weeks, beginning the first Sunday of February and ending Easter Sunday. Amplified telephones in each sanctuary broadcast the week-by-week results to each congregation.

Although one church was declared the winner, actually each church was a winner. Each church increased in average attendance by nearly 200 with their combined attendance more than 500 ahead of the pre-contest figure. Together, the three churches enrolled 731 new people in Sunday School.

In a contest of this kind, it is important to emphasize the

progress made in each church so that the losing church or churches will not be demoralized by the event. Truly, every church that grows and reaches more people than before is a winner.

5. *Special days.* A special emphasis day occasionally is good for morale and keeps the people looking forward to something. Some churches plan a special day once each quarter with a superday of some kind annually.

The secret to the success of special days is a good program and a good promotion. A letter should be sent to every person enrolled, not just every family the week prior to the occasion. Each child should receive his own letter. Some of the ideas that follow are from Jack Hyles' book *How to Boost Your Church Attendance,* Zondervan.

- *Back to School Day.* During the summer months, many of the children may have become inactive. Even the adults may need a special boost about this time of the year. Why not plan a great Back to School Day?

Recognize the children by grades, giving special acknowledgement to the grade with the most present. Make public school teachers your special guests. Have testimonies from a Christian teacher, and from elementary, junior high, and high school students.

Have students serve as ushers, bring the special music, and fill the choir. Make it a special day in honor of the students and their teachers.

It might be appropriate to invite a special guest of particular interest to the children. He could assist in a great children's rally.

Give a present to each of the students. Some churches have given pencils, ball-point pens, combs, rulers, or tablets inscribed with the church's name and a Scripture verse. All these items can be ordered at minimal cost from an advertising specialties company.

- *Round-up Day.* Early fall, in October or November, is a good time for Round-up Day. Why not have a dinner "on the grounds"? A guest music group might be a welcome attraction, bringing special music at the morning worship service and a concert Sunday afternoon.

● *Christ-in-Christmas Day.* The Sunday before Christmas is the time for Christ-in-Christmas Day. Christmas carols, a choir cantata, and a sermon on the meaning of Christmas all should be part of the program.

Perhaps a beautiful candlelight observance of the Lord's Supper could be planned for Sunday evening. A special gift or Christmas treat should be given to all the children Sunday morning.

For some, especially bus children from poorer neighborhoods, this may be the highlight of their Christmas season. Again, be sure a letter is sent to everybody enrolled, not just to member families.

● *Birthday Sunday.* Many churches have found the greatest day of all to be the church's birthday. Determine the church's anniversary date, then plan to celebrate annually that Sunday as Birthday Sunday.

A huge cake can be baked for this significant occasion. Several members can volunteer to bake "sheet cakes," which can then be assembled into a giant cake decorated by a professional cake decorator.

The cake can be in the shape of a Bible, the cross, the church building, or any other appropriate design. Following the Sunday morning worship service, plan a great fellowship meal in the church fellowship hall and eat the cake for dessert.

Special guests for this festive occasion might include a former pastor, an old or charter member, or anyone of particular interest to the people. Set a high goal for Sunday School attendance.

To promote the church's birthday, send a letter to all enrolled, enclosing a tiny birthday candle. Ask them to bring the candle to Sunday School to be used in decorating the cake. You may want to give a larger candle to every class and department that reaches its attendance goal.

• *Baby Day.* Early spring (April or May) is a good time for Baby Day. New babies have been born during the winter months. New parents may need an extra incentive to get back to the house of God. This special day is a beautiful, meaningful experience for parents and congregation alike.

The baby parade is the highlight of Baby Day. At the beginning or near the end of the morning worship service, parents go to the nursery, get their babies, and, while the organist plays "Jesus Loves Me," bring them to the front of the auditorium.

Each mother (or couple) comes to the pulpit, introduces the baby, and is given a corsage. A prayer of dedication is offered for the babies. A beautiful dedication certificate can be prepared for *each infant.*

The letter promoting Baby Day should be sent to the babies themselves. This may be the first letter they've ever received.

There is no end to special days. Old-fashioned Day, Homecoming Day, Good Neighbor Sunday, Hallelujah Sunday, Miracle Sunday, Picture-taking Sunday, Absent "T" Sunday, and scores of others have been used effectively by many churches to spark added interest and assure a larger attendance.

Someone even suggested a Someday Sunday for all those who say, "We'll be there—someday."

Of course, special days such as Christmas, Easter, Mother's Day, and Father's Day are always in the calendar. Most of these promote themselves, however, and do not need extra special attention.

A layman from First Baptist Church of Houston, Texas was asked why he felt the church had grown so rapidly and had achieved such phenomenal success. "Because," he said, "it's fun to go to church there."

It should be that way in every church. Going to church should be fun—a happy occasion, a glorious celebration.

The wise, growth-oriented pastor will not belittle effective promotional techniques. Rather, he will do everything possible to reach every person possible for Jesus.

11
How to Use Buses to Reach People

A church in Georgia was averaging 250 in attendance. Three years later this same church averaged more than 1,000 and has had as high as 1,800 on special days. There were more than 2,000 professions of faith in one year (William A. Powell, *Church Bus Evangelism,* Woodlawn Baptist Church, Decatur, Ga., pp. 18-20).

A church in Alabama had averaged 1,000 in attendance for many years. In six months, this same church saw attendance increase to nearly 2,000.

A rural church in Tennessee increased attendance from 23 to 230 in two years, while another rural Tennessee church increased from 70 to 300.

A church in Florida doubled Sunday School and worship attendance in two weeks, while another church in Georgia tripled attendance in one month.

How did they do it? At least one of the major contributing factors to these phenomenal successes was the use of buses. Although different in many ways, these churches had one thing in common—they all had an effective bus ministry.

Many churches are finding a bus ministry one of the best means of discovering prospects and reaching people for Christ.

71

Possible Disadvantages of a Bus Ministry
A bus ministry has disadvantages as well as advantages.

1. A bus ministry is expensive. Some point out that a bus ministry is expensive and will never pay for itself. That is probably true if you are thinking only of dollars and cents.

Most churches with bus ministries estimate that it costs at least $1,000 per year to operate a bus besides the initial purchase cost of the bus. But who can measure the value of a soul? And how much is it worth to have an entree into scores of homes where effective witnessing is possible and where eventually, parents can be won to Christ?

2. Riders may disturb others. Also, it has been suggested that bus riders tend to be rowdy and undisciplined, often causing disturbance and confusion. If so, this only underlines their great need for a Gospel witness and for the loving concern of someone who cares.

The truth is, many of these children look forward anxiously to Sunday School and receive a greater blessing than do some who come with adults. With little or no encouragement from home, many are up and ready, waiting for the bus every Sunday.

To be sure an unusual dedication and patience is sometimes required of workers, but certainly the reward is more than worth the toil.

3. Busing encourages parents to send rather than bring their children. It is often implied that parents will send their children on the bus rather than bring them. Actually, most pastors who have bus ministries argue that seldom, if ever, do parents who would otherwise get ready and attend with them send their children by bus. Scores of parents, who probably would never have attended otherwise, have been enlisted due to the entree to their homes through the bus ministry.

4. Busing discourages the start of a new work. One final criticism of bus ministries is that churches who have buses don't start missions, that rather than starting a mission in an unchurched area, they prefer to run a bus there.

This certainly does not need to be the case. In fact the people reached through the bus ministry can be the nucleus for a new mission. A church in New Jersey has made it a project to start both a new bus route and a new mission every year, often using the bus as a means of starting a mission.

Advantages of a Bus Ministry

Most churches that have buses believe the advantages far outweigh the several disadvantages.

1. Increases enrollment and attendance. A bus ministry may well be the one most effective way to discover new prospects and increase Sunday School enrollment and attendance. With a minimal amount of effort, workers can go door-to-door handing out materials and lining up riders.

Perhaps more people can be enlisted with less effort than in any other one way. Not only does this expand your church's Bible teaching ministry to those enlisted, but it also opens the door for an effective ministry to the parents and families of those who ride.

2. Reaches many for Christ and the church. It may be that your church can win more people to Christ through effort and money expended for the bus ministry than by any other means. Literally, thousands of people are won and baptized every year as a result of bus ministries throughout America.

Does any program sponsored by a typical church more certainly fulfill the Bible command: "Go out quickly into the streets and alleys of the town and bring in the poor, the crippled, the blind, and the lame"? (Luke 14:21, NIV)

The Bus Ministry Organization

A bus ministry will never work unless you work it. You can never just buy a bus and assume people will want to ride. Workers must be willing to go into an area, knock on doors, hand out circulars, and line up riders.

A high "dropout" rate exists among bus riders unless teachers and workers are willing to make a double effort to visit absentees and class members, provide extra class activities, and show genuine compassion and concern.

Perhaps the one great key is organization. At least five elected and trained workers are essential for every bus.

1. Bus captain. This person is in charge of the bus route. He rides the bus every Sunday, takes the roll, leads choruses and hymns, and sees that order is maintained. Riding the bus should be a learning experience for the child from the time he boards until he returns home.

Also, the bus captain contacts absentees, enlists new riders, visits the sick, strives to enlist unchurched parents and families, and generally performs pastoral duties to his small congregation. The captain's main job is to fill his bus with riders (William A. Powell, *Establishing an Aggressive Bus Ministry,* Church Growth Publications, pp. 136-149).

2. Co-captain. This person assists the captain and takes over in the captain's absence. The co-captain may be the wife or husband of the captain, or someone else assigned to the route. Often, the co-captain will be a "captain-in-training," preparing to begin or take over his own route.

3. Crusaders. Crusaders are usually teenagers who assist with bus visitation, monthly activities, and the weekly program on the bus. They ride the bus every Sunday morning and help with the singing, the records, the refreshments, and help maintain discipline.

They go to the door and help riders on and off the bus. When the bus arrives at church, they help take the children to the proper classrooms. It is well to have at least three crusaders assigned to every route (Powell, *Bus Ministry,* pp. 169-173).

4. Bus driver. Of course, every bus must have a driver. Most states do not require the driver to have a chauffeur's license. Many men or women who cannot teach, sing, or perform other ministries are fine drivers. Of course the driver must be faithful, dependable, and blessed with a pleasing personality. He must also be a skilled driver, with the safety of his riders uppermost in his mind.

BUS ORGANIZATION

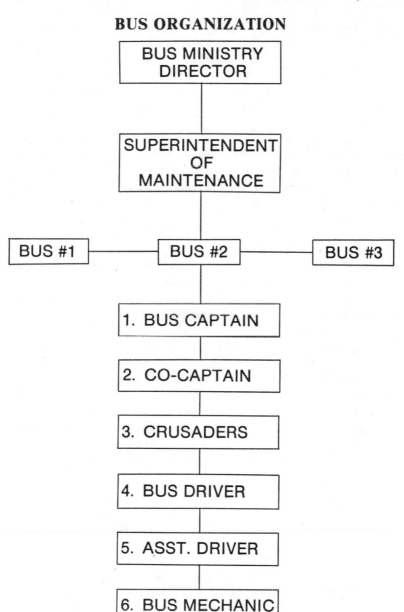

5. Assistant driver. It is essential to have an assistant driver assigned to every bus. He must be familiar with the route and ready to go on a moment's notice.

6. Bus mechanic. A mechanic should be assigned to every bus. He services the bus weekly, making any required repairs. If the driver is mechanically inclined, he can also serve as mechanic.

If the church has more than one bus, there should be a director of bus ministry who has general supervision of the entire bus program, and a superintendent of maintenance who directs the maintenance of all the buses and supervises the mechanics. The pastor should not be bothered with details related to the bus ministry.

How to Start a Bus Ministry
Assuming you decide advantages do outweigh disadvantages, what is the process whereby a bus ministry can be started?

1. Take a church vote to begin. First, the church must vote to start a bus ministry. A bus ministry may not prove a worthy project for every church. A church should be willing to make any sacrifice necessary, put up with any annoyance, and endure any frustration in order to reach more people for Christ.

If the church does not have that spirit, they may not be ready for a bus ministry. Getting the church ready may involve much preaching, teaching, and prayer. Usually, an enthusiastic pastor with a real vision of what a bus ministry can do is the key to selling the church on the idea.

2. Get a bus or buses. Second, a bus must be procured. There are several ways to get a bus.

a. Borrow a bus. Sometimes a bowling alley, skating rink, scout troup, or interested individual will lend a bus to a church. One church in Ohio was loaned two brand new buses without charge.

b. Rent or lease a bus. If a bus can be rented for $20 per Sunday or less, it will probably prove cheaper than attempting to purchase one. A bus often can be rented, with the church furnishing the driver, from a school board or local bus contractor. Again, a bowling alley, skating rink, scout troup, etc. may be possibilities.

If a bus is either leased or rented, the church always runs the risk of losing the availability of the bus with little or no advance warning. Probably, a church would be wise not to rent all their buses from one source, or to be sure other arrangements can be made for transportation quickly.

   c. Buy a bus. A third way to acquire a bus is of course, to buy it. There are many reasons why buying a bus may be preferable to renting or leasing one (Powell, *Bus Ministry,* pp. 88-96).

A bus that is owned by the church can be used for varied activities other than Sunday morning transportation. It can be used to transport people to services Sunday or Wednesday evenings, and it can be used for revivals or other spiritual activities.

The church-owned bus can be used by youth groups, mission organizations, and for class or department functions. They can be used for mission Bible schools and for housing Sunday School classes or departments.

A church in New Jersey housed more than one third of its Sunday School attendance on buses, while using other buses to shuttle classes and departments to nearby temporary facilities. Maybe owning a bus is the best way after all.

Another question often raised is: "What kind of bus should be purchased?"

In most cases, the bus should be a standard brand and should be "inspectable," that is, one that will pass your state inspection without a great deal of expense.

It is always an advantage if a bus has gone through and passed a recent inspection. Watch out for bad tires, broken glass that must be replaced, a faulty motor or transmission, and other items that will demand costly repair.

   • *Cost of a bus.* The cost of a bus may range from $1,000 to more than $15,000. Very few churches feel they have enough funds to purchase a new bus or that the limited use justifies so large an expenditure.

Probably, with careful investigation, a good road-worthy bus capable of short trips can be purchased for about $2,500. A bus good enough for in-town, Sunday-route activities only can be bought for about $1,000.

● *Financing the purchase of a bus.* Sometimes an interested donor will supply the funds to purchase a bus. Perhaps a special appeal during a worship service or a special campaign will prove successful. Some churches simply budget for the purchase of a bus.

● *Repairing and maintaining the bus.* The bus, like the church building, reflects your dedication and devotion. A shoddy, unpainted, broken-down bus leaves a bad impression. Members should take pride in their bus just as they take pride in their building.

Shortly after a bus has been purchased, it will probably need to be painted. Many churches have saved a great deal by renting or buying a paint sprayer and having the members do the work themselves. However, care should be taken to assure that professional work is done.

A skilled sign painter should paint the church name in large letters which are easy to read from a long distance. Remember, your bus is a "traveling billboard," advertising your church wherever it goes.

A bus mechanic should be assigned to every bus. Sometime during the week (probably Saturday morning), he will take the bus, service it, and make any necessary minor repairs. He will work with the other mechanics in doing major repairs necessary on any of the buses.

Parts, even tires and batteries, often can be purchased at great savings at junkyards, especially at truck salvage yards. Often, car parts, even motors, can be used to repair buses. Also, churches often can buy parts wholesale from a local distributor.

3. Enlist bus workers. After the church has voted to begin a bus ministry and a bus has been acquired, the third step is to enlist and train a bus captain. A bus captain may be anyone interested in reaching people for Christ—a college professor or a widow on a pension; a young college student or a housewife; an electronics engineer or a custodian.

The primary prerequisites are zeal, dependability, and love for people. After a captain has been enlisted, he will assist in enlisting the other workers. It is important to have a complete bus team on each bus.

4. Select a bus route location. The fourth step in starting a bus ministry is to select a possible bus route location. Where could a route be started? Perhaps, in an apartment complex, a new housing project, or a low income government housing area. Trailer courts and military bases often prove "fields white unto harvest."

Don't overlook your own immediate community. Often, scores of people who cannot be reached otherwise, and who live within a short distance of your church, can be enlisted with a bus ministry. Remember, a bus ministry is not transportation —it is evangelism.

5. Work the area. Now that a bus has been purchased, a bus route location selected, and bus workers enlisted, you are ready to work the area. It is good to take the bus captain along with other workers into the area and go door-to-door, handing out pamphlets which announce your intentions of beginning a bus route there.

The pamphlet should contain the name of your church and the bus captain, with a phone number to call, for any who want a ride. Just handing out pamphlets is not enough, however. This initial effort should be followed within a few days by a corps of workers going door-to-door, this time personally enlisting riders.

The most effective means of enlistment is a personal contact with the riders themselves. Perhaps some children are playing or loafing on a street corner. The bus captain or a worker may say, "Hello! I'm Mr. Jones. We're starting a bus route through here to Sunday School. Would you like a free bus ride every Sunday? We're trying to get 50 people to ride. Will you help us?" (Reginald M. McDonough, *Outreach with Church Buses,* Convention Press, pp. 22-27)

If the children indicate interest, the bus worker goes with them to their homes to gain the permission of their parents.

Suppose, after knocking on doors and making every effort possible to line up riders, only a few are present on your first Sunday. Don't be discouraged; with proper promotion the children themselves will be your best enlistment agents. If properly motivated to do so, they will bring their friends and soon your bus will be full.

After a route has been started, the bus captain becomes the key to sustained attendance and continued growth. Many churches demand that every bus worker give at least three or four hours every week, usually Saturday, to visiting absentees and enlisting new riders.

Problems and What to Do about Them
Someone has said, "A world without problems is an inconceivable world." Certainly, the world of the bus ministry has its problems too. Yet problems often can become opportunities if handled correctly and in the Spirit of Christ.

1. The problem of enlisting and training workers. Jesus gave the key to the problem of enlisting workers when He shared in Matthew 20 the Parable of the Husbandman who needed laborers for his vineyard and went out personally to enlist workers.

He went out the third hour, the sixth hour, the ninth hour and even the eleventh hour with the passionate plea, "'Why have you been standing here all day long doing nothing? . . . You also go and work in my vineyard'" (Matt. 20:6-7, NIV).

A successful bus ministry will demand a director of bus ministry who is willing to work hard and long at the job of enlisting workers.

Training can be achieved with special units in Training

Union or special training projects sponsored by the church. Several books, tapes, and even films on the bus ministry are available. More and more churches, associations, and state conventions are sponsoring bus clinics and conferences. Southern Baptist assemblies at Ridgecrest, North Carolina and Glorieta, New Mexico have sponsored special bus consultations.

By far, the best training and planning project would be a weekly bus workers' meeting. Many churches have found Saturday morning to be the best time for such a meeting, followed with bus visitations by bus workers and bus repair work by mechanics.

2. The problem of unruly or incorrigible riders. Harsh though it may seem, incorrigible riders who persist in disruptive, intolerable behavior and rebel against all efforts at correction, may have to be expelled from the bus ministry.

A child who persists in using profane or abusive language, skipping Sunday School, leaving the premises, fighting, disrupting a class or worship service, or acting in such a way that his conduct is intolerable, may simply be forbidden to ride.

To do otherwise is to be unfair to other students on the bus or in class who want to learn and have come to worship. Of course no such measure should be taken until every alternative has been explored and every effort possible has been made to reconcile the student.

Most bus riders are well-mannered and well-behaved. It is not right to let a few spoil it for the rest.

3. The problem of space. Many churches find that soon after a bus ministry has begun, attendance completely saturates available space. However, there are many ways to beat the space problem.

Why not use your buses to shuttle students to nearby schools, lodge halls, homes, fire halls, and other temporary quarters? You might even consider using the buses themselves for classrooms.

Multiple use of the building can be achieved with several

worship services, two or more separate Sunday Schools, or a portion of the people in Sunday School while others are in worship.

Probably the most popular method of alleviating space problems, as well as providing a more meaningful program, is the "children's church" idea.

Preschool children (0—5) are cared for with extension services. Children ages 6—9 (1—3 grades) or possibly even 6—12 (1—6 grades) have a special worship service provided for them during the regular worship hour.

Although a portion of the service might be small group activity time, it is important that the major portion be an actual worship service. If possible, an ordained minister should conduct the service, deliver the message, and offer an invitation.

Those who respond to the invitation should be dealt with carefully and prayerfully and should be thoroughly instructed as to the significance of their decision.

4. *The problem of balance.* It is most important that all who attend your church, by bus or otherwise, receive the very best in Bible teaching and worship experience. Sunday School and worship must prove a pleasing and profitable experience in order for people to continue to attend. You must not only get them there; you must also minister to their spiritual needs.

Some churches, by enthusiastic promotion of their bus ministry, soon have more in attendance than they are capable of handling effectively. Probably it is not well, in most cases, to have more than one third of your total attendance from the buses, assuming that most of the riders are teenagers and children.

The answer to the problem of balance is not to restrain the bus ministry, but rather to accelerate the effort to reach more adults. Never be satisfied until parents as well as the children have been reached.

12
How to Plan, Promote, and Conduct a Revival

The crying need of our day is revival. Anyone who visits very many churches will surely cry with the psalmist of old, "Wilt Thou not revive us again?" (Ps. 85:6)

Leonard Ravenhill pleads the cause of true, heaven-sent revival: "On the Day of Pentecost, the flame of the living God became the flame of the human heart to that glorious company. The church began with these men in the 'Upper Room' agonizing—and today is ending with men in the supper room organizing. The church began in revival; we are ending in ritual" (*Why Revival Tarries,* Bethany Fellowship, p. 161).

Much of what we call "revival" is a cheap imitation of the real thing. Many churches have "revival," they say, at least once a year. But are these protracted meetings really seasons of revival? Do carnal Christians become loving, Spirit-filled, devoted followers of Christ? Are backslidden church members sorely rebuked and sincerely convicted of their sinful ways? Do they repent and become as new? Does the "fire fall" and the church come alive? Do sinners cry out to God for salvation?

If not, there is no revival. Revival is not a series of meetings—it is a resurrection of the dead! For ". . . in Christ shall all be made alive" (1 Cor. 15:22).

If true revival prevailed in most Southern Baptist churches, would the average church baptize only 10 persons per year? Probably, the pastor alone should win that many to Christ, even if he doesn't have witnessing church members.

Leadership Is the Key
Everything rises and falls on leadership. True revival will seldom, if ever, come to a church if the pastor and the evangelist are not revived, Spirit-filled men of God. Pastor and Evangelist, what you are is more important than what you do. As E.M. Bounds has said, "The church is looking for better methods; God is looking for better men" (*Power through Prayer,* Zondervan, p. 11).

Ravenhill, himself a full-time evangelist and conference speaker, denounces cheap, money-minded pastors and evangelists with a ruthless vengeance: "Why does revival tarry? The answer is simple.... Because evangelism is so highly commercialized. The tithes of widows and the poor are spent in luxury-living by many evangelists.... Preachers, who have homes and cottages by the lake, a boat on that lake, and a big bank balance still beg for more. With such extortioners and unjust men, can God entrust Holy Ghost revival?" (*Why Revival Tarries,* pp. 44-46)

Surely this is not meant to be a wholesale indictment of all evangelists and preachers. Ravenhill certainly is aware of the scores of God-called men who labor faithfully and successfully in the field of evangelism.

But every pastor knows of the few who seem far more concerned about the love offering than the lost. Their priorities seem to be their own self-promotion and registered "decisions," no matter how superficial. Great crowds may come to be entertained and many decisions may be registered, but genuine revival will not result.

Pastors are just as guilty of these grave ills as evangelists. E.M. Bounds says: "The pulpit of this day is weak in praying. ...Prayer is with the pulpit too often only official—a performance for the routine of service. . . . Every preacher who does not make prayer a mighty factor in his own life and ministry is weak as a factor in God's work and is powerless to project God's cause. . . ." (*Power through Prayer,* p. 15)

True Revival
It can just as surely be said of true revival as it can of casting out demons: "This kind can come forth by nothing, but by prayer and fasting" (Mark 9:29).

E.M. Bounds asks a pertinent question: "Where are the Christly leaders who can teach the modern saints how to pray and put them at it? Do we know we are raising up a prayerless set of saints? Where are the apostolic leaders who can put God's people to praying? Let them come to the front and do the work, and it will be the greatest work that can be done" (*Power through Prayer,* p. 85).

The formula for true revival is simple, but that doesn't mean it is easy. It remains unchanged throughout the ages: "If My people, which are called by My name, shall humble themselves, and pray, and seek My face, and turn from their wicked ways; then will I hear from heaven, and will forgive their sin, and will heal their land" (2 Chron. 7:14).

If true revival is so utterly dependent on God, is there any need or place for planning and preparation? Should you not simply tarry and pray, and wait for the "fire to fall"?

No, this is not God's way. Many would like it to be, for little effort would then be required and small sacrifice would need to be made. The blood of souls stains the hands of those who let their sham "spirituality" excuse their lazy indifference.

God always works His miracles through prepared people. He prepared His people for the Land of Promise in Moses' day. He organized them by companies, set leaders in their midst, and then the fire fell (Ex. 18:13-26; 19:18). He prepared them to inherit the land by commanding them to "sanctify themselves" and follow their spiritual leaders into the waters (Josh. 3:1-17).

Before Pentecost, the disciples agonized (Acts 1:14) and

organized (Acts 1:23). After the fire fell, they advertised (Acts 2:6) and evangelized (Acts 2:14-36; 40). Is it any different today? If these early apostles felt the need to plan and promote, as well as pray, can you do otherwise? Perhaps a rather familiar cliche is appropriate: "Pray as if everything depended on God; work as though everything depended on you."

Consider some helpful techniques which may be of value in planning, promoting, and conducting a revival campaign.

1. Appoint a revival campaign committee. Enlist a revival campaign committee to help you plan, promote, and prepare for the special meetings. Let the committee represent a cross section of the church family. Old and young, men and women, rich and poor should all be represented. In some cases the church council might function as this committee if it has a real burden for true revival.

What are the duties of this committee? They will consider important matters such as precampaign prayer services, publicity, transportation to the revival meetings, hospitality for the campaign team, attendance plans, special nights and events, and many other pertinent matters. Of course, if the evangelist has sent along a campaign plan sheet or suggested ideas, the committee should work diligently to carry out these plans.

The committee should have its first meeting about six months prior to the scheduled revival. Every matter suggested above should be carefully considered and job assignments made to appropriate individuals. Then the committee should meet when necessary to check these assignments and be sure that the plans are being implemented.

2. Organize prayer efforts. Prayer is the one most important ingredient in any true revival. Don't neglect this important matter. Challenge your people to remember the campaign in prayer, constantly and continually. Urge them to make prayer lists of lost and backslidden persons and pray for them daily.

• *Round-the-clock prayers.* For the 24 hours preceding the first service of the revival, have one or several in the church at the altar on their knees praying for revival. Day and night, for

24 hours, they should pray. A prayer clock may be constructed with different persons signed up for different periods of the day and night.

A less effective variation is to let the people pray at home, at work, or wherever they may be. Regardless of how it is done, saturate the revival effort with prayer.

• *Prayer fellowships.* The "cottage prayer service" idea still remains a mighty source of revival power. Here members get together in the intimacy of someone's home for old-fashioned, on-their-knees prayer for revival.

• *Preservice prayer groups.* It is well to have groups of people praying prior to the service each evening. Why not have men meeting in one place, women another, and youth in yet another with a leader for each group? Pray specifically and by name for the lost, the unchurched, the backslidden, the revival campaign team, and the meetings in general.

3. Select and promote a revival campaign theme. A campaign theme, such as "Lord, Send a Revival," "Let's Just Praise the Lord," "Jesus Never Fails," or "Revive Us Again" can be used and will add interest and purpose to the meeting.

It is great if an appropriate song can be selected to help support the theme. Also, it is good to have a large banner hanging across the front of the church promoting the revival theme.

4. Advertise and promote the revival campaign. "It pays to advertise" is an ancient adage, but also a profound truth. One reason there was such a large crowd on the Day of Pentecost was because "this was noised abroad" (Acts 2:6).

• *The local newspaper.* Prepare an attractive news release for the local papers. Usually, the newspapers will print a good story with a picture if it is prepared in proper form. Use a few brief announcements before the meetings, then a good feature story at the beginning of the campaign.

• *Radio and TV stations.* Attractive news releases should be prepared for all local radio and TV stations. Always make original copies; never send carbons or Xeroxed copies. It is best to deliver releases by hand, meeting the news editor personally and answering any questions he may have.

Although they may deny it, many radio, TV, and newspaper officials will give better news coverage if you also purchase advertising space. When time and space are limited, it is logical that preference should be given to paid advertisers.

• *Paid advertisements.* Again, it pays to advertise. Good promotion, however done, is not a cost; it is an investment that returns great dividends. Buy an ad in the newspaper—maybe even spot announcements on TV and radio.

• *Printed circulars.* Print some attractive circulars with pictures of the revival team. Much good can come from printed circulars.

Enlist a group of youth, a Royal Ambassador Chapter, or a children's department to pass out circulars door-to-door through your community. After the job is complete, take them out for a treat. It will be money well spent.

Also, circulars can be hung in store windows, sent by mail to prospects, used as bulletin inserts, and made available to your people for distribution.

• *Letters to members.* A letter promoting the revival campaign and urging faithful attendance should be sent to every member family. Perhaps you should send several letters, one each week for three weeks prior to the meeting. Also, it is well to send a letter the week of the campaign itself, with a love offering envelope urging the family's contribution to the revival effort.

• *Letters to prospects.* Another letter, promoting the revival campaign, should be sent to all prospects. Be sure to include a campaign circular. (A much less effective alternative is simply to address one of the circulars and send it.)

5. *Have visitation before and during revival meetings.* All the signs, banners, ads, and circulars in the world cannot take the place of the personal touch.

Did you hear what happened to the soldier who wrote his girlfriend 300 letters in 300 days while in the service? He came home and found she had married the mailman! Yes, visitation does make a difference.

Some good approaches for revival visitation might include:

• *A visitation blitz.* Why not have an after-church "visitation blitz" the Sunday before the revival campaign begins? Prepare a light lunch for the people. While they are eating, make visitation assignments. Plan to visit every known prospect, urge his attendance during the campaign, and witness to the unsaved.

• *A telephone blitz.* A variation of the visitation blitz is a "telephone blitz." Give out prospect cards during the Sunday morning worship service with simple instructions. Have the people make a telephone visit to every prospect, urging attendance at the revival. Also, member family cards can be handed out.

• *Visitation each day during the revival campaign.* If you have morning services, ask those attending to make at least one visit on the way home. Have fresh prospect cards ready for those who volunteer.

Surely, the revival team should expect to spend at least three hours each day in personal visitation.

6. *Have special nights and events during the revival campaign.* Many churches like to plan a series of special nights during the revival campaign, such as Family Night, Youth Night, Sunday School Night, Men's Night, Ladies' Night, Old-fashioned Night, etc.

Sometimes these special nights can be preceded with a special activity or event, such as Men's Fellowship Supper on Men's Night, Hamburger Fry or Pizza Party on Youth Night, Hot Dog Supper on Children's Night.

All this takes work, costs money, and demands much time and effort. It costs to reach people. Is it worth it? Jesus asks, "For what shall it profit a man, if he shall gain the whole world, and lose his own soul? Or what shall a man give in exchange for his soul?" (Mark 8:36-37)

Apparently, Jesus felt one soul was worth more than the

entire world! Surely then, a soul is worth more than a hot dog or a piece of pizza! Surely, a soul is worth the money it takes to buy an ad in the paper or put a spot on the radio. Surely, a soul is worth the effort it takes to assign a pew to someone each evening.

7. *Use the best attendance-getter of all.* Full-time evangelist Clyde Chiles said: "All other revival plans combined are not as effective as 'pack-a-pew.'" He was only echoing the sentiment of most other evangelists and pastors alike. This old favorite attendance-getter remains a favorite with the evangelistic pastor and the growing church.

"Pack-a-pew" or some similar concept is essential for good, sustained attendance. Even the most dynamic preacher will not, in most cases, keep a full house every night, but the personal touch will. When every pew is assigned to someone every night, and the assignee faithfully does his task, you can be sure of a good attendance and a great revival campaign.

Does revival really contribute to church growth? Church growth expert Donald McGavran questions a casual relationship between revival and growth:

"Revival bears a close relationship to church growth; yet exactly what that relationship is . . . is often not clear. Under certain conditions revival may be said to cause growth. Under others, its relationship to church growth is so distant that apparently revival occurs without growth and growth without revival" (*Understanding Church Growth,* Eerdmans, p. 163).

Be that as it may, a good look at churches and denominations that have long ago ceased having revival campaigns convinces even the skeptical of the value of revival meetings. The prayer of every sincere Christian should be that of the Prophet Habakkuk, "O Lord, revive Thy work. . . ." (Hab. 3:2)

13
How to Use
Saturation Evangelism

Gary Holder, minister of evangelism for the First Baptist Church, of Dallas, Texas, defines saturation evangelism as "reaching anybody, anywhere, anytime for Christ." The innovative mind will imagine many and varied ways to implement this principle.

Jesus was the first to advocate and command saturation evangelism. In the Great Commission, He said: "Go into all the world and preach the Good News to all creation" (Mark 16:15, NIV). "All the world" surely means "everywhere"; "to every creature" certainly means "everybody."

No church has fulfilled the Great Commission until every person in its community has heard the Gospel. All may not have received Jesus, but at least they have all been "evangelized."

The Great Commission transcends all barriers. Racial, social, and economical barriers come tumbling down as the true New Testament church fulfills its "marching orders." The growing church takes seriously the Lord's command and is not satisfied until every person, regardless of race, age, or economic situation, has heard the Gospel.

The church that pitches its ministry to a select few or a

sophisticated elite cannot expect the blessing of God. Selective evangelism is the very antithesis of saturation evangelism and is not worthy of the name *Christian.*

Homogeneous Unit

Some authors have made much of what has been called the "homogeneous unit" principle. They believe every church tends to become a "homogeneous unit," made up of people of similar kinds.

Perhaps churches, like people, do tend to develop particular personalities. Likes do attract and any church is apt to reach certain people more effectively than others. Nevertheless, the mandate of the Great Commission falls squarely on every church: "Preach the Gospel to every creature."

It is not the prerogative of any church to ignore that clear command. No church is truly New Testament, no matter how sound its doctrine, until that Commission is literally fulfilled in its life and community.

Some persons are reached by church expansion (church growth), while others are reached by church extension (mission congregations, branch Sunday Schools, extension Bible classes). One way or another, all much be reached.

It is the task of the church to design an outreach program which will fulfill the Great Commission to take the Gospel to every creature. Each person in your community should have the Gospel presented to him forcefully and frequently.

Many churches confuse purpose with goals. The goal of a church may well be to increase attendance, double enrollment, or add so many new members. These are worthy goals, but they are not the purpose of the church. Unless the members clearly understand the purpose of the church, goals and efforts to reach these goals will have little meaning.

Church Purpose

What is the purpose of the church? Howard Ball, director of Churches Alive, states emphatically that the purpose of a New

Testament church is to fulfill the Great Commission. When the members clearly understand this overarching purpose, it will bring meaning to everything they seek to do.

We seek to increase attendance, double baptisms, and add members, not so we can boast of bigger numbers, but so we can more completely fulfill the Commission. The most effective way to "preach the Gospel to every creature" is to get people within the walls of the church building where the Gospel is faithfully taught and preached every Sunday.

But many remain outside the walls, despite our finest efforts to bring them in. However, they still remain within the scope of our Commission. We cannot discharge our responsibility simply because they will not come to our church building. A sign in the churchyard, an ad in the newspaper, or even a personal invitation does not free us from our mandate: "Preach the Gospel to every creature."

No man, black or white, must escape our witness. Neither the richest baron nor the poorest child should be able to live in our community without having clearly heard the claims of the Gospel and the plan of salvation. This is the Lord's command to His church.

Reach the Outsider

How then, can we effectively communicate the Gospel, especially to those who never come within our walls?

1. A mission congregation. Though some within the church's community may not come to the church, this must not hinder the church from going to them. Though they should always be welcome, black people do not always feel comfortable in a white church. In order to fulfill the Great Commission, the church may need to start a mission congregation with black leadership.

Those of another ethnic, cultural, or economic background may feel shut out of the typical WASP (white Anglo-Saxon Protestant) congregation. Try as it may, the church may be frustrated in its efforts to reach these groups by church expansion. Church extension is probably the most effective approach.

The church should never attempt a mission project because it does not want to reach certain people for its own congregation. Any such motivation is unworthy and ungodly. The Lord will never bless if the motive for starting the new work is anything less than a sincere effort to reach the most people possible in the best possible way.

2. Branch Sunday Schools. Many churches can reach persons in a particular area of their community with extension Sunday Schools. Using their own members to staff the schools, the churches can branch out into the inner city, the ethnic areas, or the economically deprived sections.

The schools can be held Sunday mornings at the traditional 9:30 hour, or may better be held in the afternoon or some evening through the week. In this way the same workers used in the main school can staff the branch school, if need be. The church buses can be used and even some of the church staff can be available.

Where can the branch school be held? Find an abandoned church building and rent it. Find an empty storefront and lease it. Use a lodge hall, a fire hall, a vacant house, a church bus, a school building, a home, or a garage.

Should attendance in mission and branch Sunday Schools be counted in your regular report? Certainly. It is a legitimate part of your church's Bible-teaching program.

3. Backyard Bible clubs. During the summer months, young people can be kept busy every day conducting Bible clubs in parks, playgrounds, backyards (or better yet, front yards), vacant lots, a garage, or an alley. Always there's a place just waiting to be used. Backyard Bible clubs should be planned every summer for every area of your community.

Remember, your orders are to "preach the Gospel to every creature." In the summer of 1977, Tower Grove Baptist Church in St. Louis planned and conducted 20 Bible clubs, enrolling more than 1,500 children.

A backyard Bible Club is designed to last about 90 minutes a day, Monday through Friday. The program includes games, a Bible story, a missionary story, and refreshments. Excellent materials detailing every activity are available from several publishers, including the Baptist Sunday School Board, Nashville, Tennessee.

To promote and advertise the club, it is well to print free tickets announcing the time and location. About one hour before the scheduled starting time, workers should go through the neighborhood, giving tickets to the children. While the children are arriving, conduct planned games and activities.

Bible clubs can be used to start or strengthen bus routes. On the last day, ask those who do not attend Sunday School anywhere to sign up on the bus that goes through that community. In this way children reached temporarily through the club will become part of the ongoing program.

4. *The Gospel movie bus.* Lafayette Park Baptist Church in St. Louis may have been the first to develop the "movie bus" idea. In the summer of 1971, the church enrolled 2,436 children in a six-week period.

Tower Grove Baptist Church, St. Louis, also uses the movie bus effectively. In the summer of 1977, more than 1,000 were enrolled on the bus in the Tower Grove community, and 50 made professions of faith.

The movie bus can be any old bus brightly painted and equipped with a screen. The screen is mounted near the front, and a projector sits on a small table at the rear of the bus. Of course the movie bus can be used only at night, unless provision is made to darken the interior. For electricity to run the projector, simply ask someone for permission to plug into an outlet.

All kinds of movies can be borrowed from a local library or rented from a film distributor. A simple 15-minute cartoon should be included in the program. This draws a crowd and helps the children have a happy time.

Following the movie workers share their testimonies and

explain the plan of salvation. Those who indicate interest are invited to remain where they are, to be personally counseled by a worker.

Don't forget to sign them up for a church bus if one regularly comes to that area. One of the greatest benefits of the movie bus is enlisting new riders for a bus route.

5. *Community programs.* Puppet shows, magic rallies, a clown performance, or the appearance of a music group are all ways of attracting a crowd, presenting the Gospel, enlisting bus riders, and fulfilling the Great Commission. Send the workers in ahead of time, give out free tickets, and wait for the crowd.

Use your youth choir or special music groups in "Operation Sing-Sing" to share a witness in shopping centers or other places where great crowds gather. "Be as shrewd as snakes and as innocent as doves" (Matt. 10:16, NIV). Do what you have to do to make certain the Gospel is shared with every person.

6. *Home Bible study fellowships.* Home Bible study fellowships have become, in recent years, a popular means of extending the church's ministry. Neighbors who might never enter the church building will gladly come to a friend's home for Bible study.

A Bible study fellowship may be held anywhere and anytime. It may be in the morning for the ladies or in the evening for the entire family. Many churches have developed from such fellowships; often, however, they are simply a means of sharing the Gospel.

Helpful materials are available from publishing houses, but the best material is the Bible itself. Resist the temptation to hand out materials prepared and copyrighted by some denomination. These materials may offend the student and kill the Bible study. Teach from the open Bible.

Can students attending home Bible studies be counted in the church's regular attendance report? Certainly. Again this is a legitimate, commendable part of your church's Bible-teaching program. However, it is important that only church-selected teachers be used.

Many other methods can and should be used in saturation evangelism. The creative, innovative person will think of many in addition to the ones cited here. Remember, you are not really a New Testament church until you have sought to "preach the Gospel to every creature."

14

How to Plan, Promote, and Conduct a Bible School

Perhaps greater church growth can be achieved in a shorter time with Bible School than any other means. As much time is spent in Bible study in a two-week school as in six months of regular attendance in Sunday School. One out of every three unsaved children enrolled will be won to Christ in that brief time (J.N. Barnette, *The Pull of the People,* Convention Press, p. 6).

Like everything else, successful Bible Schools don't just happen. They take much toil, sweat, and tears. But how much is it worth to reach a child for Christ in the formative, impressionable years of his life? How much is it worth to your church to reach many more people, not only for a week or two of Vacation Bible School, but hopefully for the ongoing program as well?

Seven Priorities
At least seven things contribute to the success of a Bible School.

1. Effective promotion and publicity. Several weeks before the school begins, a concerted effort to publicize the school should be conducted using signs and banners, posters, handbills, news releases in local newspapers and on radio, and sending letters to every child who is enrolled in your Sunday School.

One of the best methods of advertising the school is to plan some exciting events during the school, such as the appearance of a clown, a magic show, a puppet performance, etc., then build publicity around the events. For example, the circular advertising the Bible School may carry a picture of the magician or the clown.

Also, news releases in the local paper can feature a picture of the magician, clown, or other attraction. Remember, "a picture is worth a thousand words," especially with children and youth. Attractive circulars advertising the school should be passed out to every house in your community.

Be sure a phone number is given to be called if transportation is needed. Be sure your buses are ready to pick up riders during VBS. Perhaps nothing will strengthen your bus routes more than an effective VBS.

Children (perhaps an older children's department, bus riders, or a young people's group) can help you distribute the circulars. It is best if they knock at each door and seek to enlist other children, getting the names and addresses of those who need rides. This should be done on Friday or Saturday before the school begins. Take those who help to a local fast-food restaurant for a hamburger and soft drink.

A letter promoting the school should be sent to every older preschooler, child, and youth enrolled in Sunday School. (Be sure the letter is sent to the child himself and not to the family.) You may want to enlist some young people to help you address envelopes.

Enclose a free ticket to Bible School with a place for the child's name, address, and phone number. The ticket, then, serves as a pre-enrollment card.

Other means of promoting the school might include a large sign in the front yard of the church, large signs on the side of each bus, posters in store windows (have a poster contest to motivate children and youth to make posters) and, of course, a great parade.

2. Pre-enrollment of students. The Sunday one week prior to the beginning of the VBS should be designated "Pre-enrollment Sunday." Sunday School workers should seek to pre-enroll every preschooler, child, and youth who is present. The following week the workers should contact everyone who was not present and seek to pre-enroll him. Also, they should seek to pre-enroll all prospects.

3. Parade Day. What some have called "Preparation Day" might better be called "Parade Day." Usually, this is the Friday or Saturday before the school begins on Monday. It is a day of practice and preparation (practice the march-in and the songs used in the joint worship program), of pre-enrollment of students so that you will not need to take time for this on the first day of the school, and of promoting the school throughout the community.

After the preliminaries have been completed, students should prepare for the grand parade. Leading the parade is a motorcycle policeman followed by a clown on a motorcycle escorting the "king" and "queen" in a lovely convertible. Then follows Uncle Elmer and Cousin Betsy, dressed as hillbillies, in a Model T.

Following these are more convertibles filled with children and church buses loaded with enthusiastic, singing, shouting riders (Jack Hyles, *How to Boost Your Church Attendance,* Zondervan, p. 87 ff.).

Of course, large banners advertising the school are posted on the sides of each bus. As the parade proceeds through the community, fliers advertising the school are given to on-lookers. The parade ends up back at the church or a nearby park where ice cream is served to everyone.

4. Promotional program each day during the VBS. The last 15 minutes of the school each day can be used for a closing assembly to promote the school from day-to-day. As students march into the auditorium from their departments, have them sing choruses and hymns. (Be careful that songs are not so stimulating that the children become unruly.)

Then, recognize every student who brought another with him to Bible School. (You may want to give "Brought One" buttons to everyone who brought someone, while the group sings "Bring Them In.")

Then comes the crowning of the king and queen, the boy and the girl who brought the most people. While the organist plays "Pomp and Circumstance," the king and queen are seated on their thrones (use chairs with sheets over them). The following day the king and queen serve as flagbearers.

The closing assembly each day includes a special feature (appearance of a clown, policeman, fireman, etc., but always with a testimony) and a message in magic from "Sardini, the Gospel Magician." This 15-minute closing program may do more to build attendance than everything else combined.

5. Gigantic picnic the last day of school. Did you ever see a child who didn't get excited about a picnic? A well-planned, rousing picnic will do much to promote the school and assure its success. When should the picnic be held? Probably on the last day of the school. Children may bring sack lunches and the picnic can be held at noon following the last day's activities.

Of course, you should do everything possible to make this a gala affair, with clowns, relays, contests, ice cream, etc. (One pastor tried to sky-dive into a park but ended up in the duck pond!)

By all means, be sure parents are invited to the picnic. Make a special effort to meet the parents and make them feel welcome.

6. Parents' Service on Sunday morning. The tragedy of many Bible Schools is that most of those enrolled are never enlisted in the ongoing Bible-teaching program. To counteract this, many churches have the Parents' Service on Sunday morning rather than Friday or Saturday evening.

This gives Bible School students and their parents an opportunity to see the church in action on Sunday morning and gives the Sunday School workers an opportunity to meet these students and enroll them in Sunday School. Also, it will almost assure the highest Sunday School attendance of the entire year.

Assuming your Sunday School begins at 9:30 A.M., students go to the appropriate Sunday School area (in most cases this is probably the. same room where they were in Bible School). VBS workers are in charge for this particular Sunday. They introduce the regular Sunday School workers, tell about Sunday School, seek to enroll new members, and take records on all who are present.

Adults meet in a general assembly in the church auditorium. Sunday School workers are introduced and someone, probably the pastor, leads a Bible study.

At 10:00 A.M., children and youth line up for the march-in. (A special area of the auditorium is reserved for them.) Parents participate in the joint worship service, in which each department presents a three-to-five minute feature. The pastor delivers the commencement address (sermon) and gives an invitation. An open house may follow.

7. *Prospect follow-up.* The enrollment cards from Bible School are probably the best prospect cards you have; go to work on them immediately (Barnette, *Pull of the People,* p. 13). The week following Bible School, a concerted effort should be made to visit the parents of every child enrolled in VBS.

Seek to enlist those who are not attending church regularly. If the parents prove "unenlistable," seek to enlist the children and have them ready to ride the bus the following Sunday. Any child who is not attending somewhere regularly should be personally contacted and enlisted on one of the bus routes.

Sunday School should be promoted each day during Bible School. Try to get the children excited about attending Sunday School. You may wish to plan a trip, a picnic, or special event for those who attend Sunday School and promote this during Vacation Bible School.

Be Prepared

Will you be ready for the great crowds who come to Bible School? Will you have enough space for them? Will there be an adequate number of departments and classes? Will you have enough workers? If not, all your efforts to increase attendance may prove worse than useless. Your good promotion may prove to be your worst enemy as your VBS degenerates into confusion and chaos.

Think big! Plan toward a great school with many in attendance. If necessary plan to use nearby buildings, such as schools or fire halls, for additional space. Actually, many classes can meet under shade trees on the church lawn or in the church buses.

For extra workers, you might consider using older youth as helpers and providing a "Teen Times" VBS later. Also, unsaved or unchurched parents can be used as group leaders, but not as teachers. This may get them involved and help you reach them for Christ.

Of course, a great Bible School requires the help of all ablebodied members, both men and women. Be sure adequate training has been provided for all your workers.

Is it worth it? A Bible School will provide as many hours of Bible teaching as several months of regular attendance in Sunday School. More people are saved in a shorter time in VBS than anywhere else. Thousands are reached every year through VBS who would never be reached otherwise.

You cannot neglect the command and promise given in Proverbs 22:6: "Train up a child in the way he should go; and when he is old, he will not depart from it."

15
How to Follow Up on Those Reached

Certainly, outreach should be a top priority in the life of any New Testament church. Just as important as reaching people and winning them to Christ, however, is the matter of developing them in their faith and witness.

D.L. Moody reportedly said, "I would rather train 10 soul-winners than win 10 souls." He rightfully concluded that our task is never done until the saved are growing in the Lord and are getting people saved. Perhaps this can be called "inreach."

The following are some methods a church can use to aid new members (and old members) in their spiritual growth.

In-depth Counseling at the Altar
At every service have the deacons come forward at the invitation to counsel with any who make decisions. These deacons must be trained in dealing with the unsaved, the backslidden, those transferring membership, etc. The deacons counsel from the open Bible, those who have made decisions, pray with them, and assure them in their commitment.

No one should simply be asked to "fill out a card!" Everyone should be dealt with thoroughly and personally, and everything possible done to assure that his decision is meaningful and real (Mack R. Douglas, *How to Build an Evangelistic Church,* Zondervan, p. 81).

Guided Bible Study

Those who come forward—adults, youth, or children—should be given a Bible study booklet to guide them in meaningful studies in such pertinent subjects as the Christian experience, prayer, the Spirit-filled life, etc. This is a "fill-in-the-blank" type booklet with five study lessons on these various subjects.

You may wish to use the SBC materials entitled *New Church Member Training Workbook for Adults, New Church Member Training Workbook for Youth,* and *New Church Member Training Workbook for Children,* published by the Baptist Sunday School Board. These can be ordered from the Church Materials Department, Baptist Sunday School Board, 127 Ninth Avenue North, Nashville, Tennessee 37234.

New Member Orientation Classes for All Ages

An appropriate person (perhaps the pastor or pastor's wife) should teach a class for all new adult members during Training Union time on Sunday evenings. The class continues for five weeks and graduates are awarded a certificate. Another person should teach a class for new members, grades 1—6, on Sunday morning during Sunday School. Also, a class should be held for youth.

Staff Conference with Every New Member

Shortly after a new member joins the church, the pastor or one of the ministers should visit in that new member's home for a personal conference. A profile sheet or member survey card should be filled out for the church files.

The profile sheet contains pertinent information such as past church work experience, special skills or talents, and particular interests or needs. (This becomes a file of potential workers for the organizations.)

Seek to involve every member, as soon as possible, in some

kind of church responsibility. People grow faster, study more, and are more faithful if they are involved in a place of personal service.

Deacon Visit to Every New Member

Shortly after a new member joins, a deacon should visit the home. The deacon has a packet of pertinent materials, including tracts on prayer, the Spirit-filled life, Bible study, etc., and copies of the church budget, a recent financial report, and a church brochure.

The deacon should go over this material with the new member and let him know he (the deacon) is available in any time of need, day or night. Of course, both deacon and staff should seek to win to Christ any member of the family who is unsaved.

Deacon-led Family Ministry Plan

Every member of the church should be assigned to a deacon. He will be the deacon-sponsor for the member's family. Each deacon has about 20 families in his zone. The deacon visits at least 2 of his families every week, thus visiting each family several times each year.

He also visits them immediately in time of death, sickness, or crisis, and is on call anytime, day or night. As already mentioned, he visits the new members in his zone the week they join the church.

Complete materials for the deacon-led family ministry plan have been prepared by the Church Administration Department of the Baptist Sunday School Board and are available through the Baptist bookstores.

These materials include the deacon notebook, the family card, the monthly report card, the referral card (used if deacon needs to refer a person to the pastor or someone else), and a pamphlet explaining how to set up and operate the family ministry plan (Howard B. Foshee, *The Ministry of the Deacon,* Convention Press, pp. 84-89; 95-99).

New Member Banquet and Program

Once each quarter, it is good to have a banquet welcoming new members. Old members come, bringing enough food for their own family plus an additional family. Of course new members and their families are honored guests and are not required to bring food. (New members, grades 1—6, should bring a parent.)

The staff, including the pastor, serves the meal as old and new members mingle in a great time of fellowship. Following the meal, each staff member gives a 10-minute résumé of his duties and promotes his particular ministry. After the program, there should be a time of fun and directed recreation.

New Member Sponsor Program

The new member sponsor program includes assigning every new member to a mature member for cultivation and follow-up. Hopefully, the new member sponsor can live in the near vicinity of the new member, and be of the same sex and age.

Ideally, the new member sponsor becomes a real and personal friend, and not just a sponsor. Of course, someone has to be assigned the responsibility of selecting sponsors every week, of sending a letter informing them of their assignments, and of receiving their reports.

The letter instructs the sponsor to: (1) visit the new member every week for four weeks and at least once a month for six months; (2) invite the new member to the sponsor's home for a meal and for fellowship; (3) offer to provide transportation to church for Sunday School, Training Union, or worship services. The letter also contains three self-addressed, postage-paid report cards to be returned, one at the end of the first week, one at the end of the first month, and one at the end of six months (Douglas, *Evangelistic Church,* pp. 85-86). (See Appendix.)

Automatic Enrollment in Sunday School

Perhaps the greatest organization for new member follow-up and cultivation is a vital Sunday School class and department.

An enrollment card should be filled out on every new member the week he joins and the appropriate Sunday School worker should contact the new member immediately. With his consent, he is automatically enrolled in Sunday School.

All of these methods, and more, are needed if you are to successfully disciple the new convert and nurture him in his faith and witness. You should do everything necessary, and all that is possible, to help him grow in the Lord.

16
The Last Word in Church Growth

The Lord Jesus gave the last word in church growth when He declared in John 15:5, "Without Me, you can do nothing." Notice, He did not say, "Without Me you can't do much," or "You can't do anything very well." Jesus boldly declares, "Without Me you can do nothing."

No concept is more widely debated or thoroughly studied among theologians than the matter of church growth. Scores of books have been written and research projects undertaken. Seminaries have established special departments and even separate schools on the subject. Courses on church growth are offered on campus and on cassette tape while church growth bulletins and periodicals abound.

Many such efforts have tended to refine church growth to a social science which rigidly adheres to certain laws of growth. These laws, supposedly, determine the progress or failure of the church's outreach.

As one reads these books or listens to the so-called experts, he sometimes finds himself wondering, "Where does God fit in? Is there no place for a vital ministry of the Holy Spirit? Can simple formulas and scientific laws really assure church growth, with or without the blessing of God?"

"Unless the church is a homogeneous unit, it will not grow," declares one authority.

"Ten will be enrolled and five in attendance for every worker enlisted," says another.

"It's strictly a numbers game," observes yet another. "For every 18 visits made, there will be at least 1 addition."

Lest one be deceived by such assertions, it is time again to hear the last word in church growth: "Without Me, you can do nothing."

What true churchman has not discovered long ago the absolute futility of refining successful ministry to such simple formulas? Just as certainly as one can detect the vast difference between the anointed man of God, the one who attempts to minister in the flesh, so one quickly observes when God's blessing is not upon a method or technique.

What pastor has not suffered the frustration of seeing a pet program or plan come to utter failure, while the same, in another place or another time, was greatly blessed? What evangelist has not, time and again, seen the same plans utterly fail in one place and gloriously blessed in another?

A pastor and church may resolve to diligently apply these learned techniques, which have proved so effective elsewhere. With great effort, they set about to implement these plans. "It worked there; surely it will work here." But alas, no results.

Another church seems to violate every principle that applies to effective outreach: The congregation breaks cultural barriers, the building is inadequate, classes and departments are too large, the program does not seem of superior quality—yet the church grows.

And now, here is yet another book telling you how to do it. Hopefully, there is much practical help and many good suggestions within these pages. However, anyone attempting to implement every idea will surely court disaster. Only the Holy Spirit can lead you in knowing what is right and workable in your particular situation.

You may find no real answer to this dilemma, except to

acknowledge the sovereignty of God. He gives "just as He determines" (1 Cor. 12:11, NIV). In His providence and election alone, a church must rest its cause. "Without Me, you can do nothing."

APPENDIX

DR LARRY L LEWIS, Pastor
REV GARY HOLDER, Associate Pastor
MR BOB MURPHY, Minister of Music
REV DARRELL ELLSWORTH, Minister To Deaf
REV FELIX WILLIAMS, Mission Pastor
DR JOE PEWETT, Counselor
MS JANORA SKEENS Childrens Director
MR WAYNE LANIER Minister of Youth and Recreation

Tower Grove
BAPTIST CHURCH

TOWER GROVE and MAGNOLIA, ST. LOUIS, MISSOURI, 63110
314/776-6446

"SERVING CHRIST IN SAINT LOUIS AND AROUND THE WORLD"

Dear Member:

A new Christian needs help! He is trying to break old habits and un-
wholesome friendships, and take up an entirely new way of life. The devil
is trying to discourage him. Doubts and questions plague his mind. He
needs a friend! Someone who will help him get his feet on the ground.
Someone who will encourage, advise, and direct him in this new way of life.
Someone who will be a _real_ friend!

Seeing this need, our church voted recently to start a new member adoption
plan. _Every new member of our church is being assigned to one of our older_
members. I trust you will be happy to participate in this worthy program.

The new member assigned to you is:

    Name: _____

    Address: _____   Phone: _____

If you cannot agree to serve as sponsor for this new member, please notify me
immediately so he may be assigned to someone else! Here are things you are
to do to help this person along:

    1. Visit in his home immediately and frequently. May I suggest you make
    at least one visit a week for the next four weeks, then at least one visit
    per month for the next six months. "Talk up" the church and try to en-
    courage him to participate in the total program.

    2. Invite him to your home, perhaps for coffee, or even a meal. Set a
    specific time, not merely a general invitation.

    3. Invite him to ride with you to Training Union and mid-week service.
    Do everything you can to enlist him in every organization of the church!

    4. Be a friend--a _real_ friend! Do not tell him you have been chosen to
    be his sponsor. Go as a friend, not as a sponsor!

I feel only a few in our church are qualified to do this work well. You are
one of them. I can't emphasize enough how important this is. Please do not
let me, or this new Christian, down.

                                        In Christ,

                                        Larry Lewis, Pastor

LL:nb

114

NEW MEMBER SPONSOR REPORT CARDS
Report #1
(to be returned within 1 week)

Dear Pastor: Name: _____

   I have called on the new member assigned to me. Here is my report:

__Has been working on New Members Bible Study	Yes__	No__
(given to new converts when they come forward)		
__Plans to attend Sunday School	Yes__	No__
__Plans to attend Training Union	Yes__	No__
__Plans to attend mid-week and worship service	Yes__	No__
__Has problem and needs Pastor	Yes__	No__

  Comments: _____

_____

            Signed: _____

Report #2
(to be returned after 1 month)

Dear Pastor: Name: _____

   I have called on the new member assigned to me _____ times. Here is my report:

__Attends Sunday School regularly	Yes__	No__
__Attends Training Union regularly	Yes__	No__
__Attends mid-week and worship services	Yes__	No__
__Has daily Bible reading and prayer	Yes__	No__
__Is witnessing to others	Yes__	No__
__Seems to be growing in Christ	Yes__	No__
__Has problem and needs Pastor	Yes__	No__

  Comments: _____

_____

            Signed: _____

Report #3
(to be returned after 2 months)

Dear Pastor: Name: _____

   I have called on the new member assigned to me _____ times. Here is my report:

__Attends Sunday School regularly	Yes__	No__
__Attends Training Union regularly	Yes__	No__
__Attends mid-week and worship services	Yes__	No__
__Has daily Bible reading and prayer	Yes__	No__
__Is witnessing to others	Yes__	No__
__Seems to be growing in Christ	Yes__	No__
__Has problem and needs Pastor	Yes__	No__

  Comments: _____

_____

            Signed: _____

Reach Out
Prospect Assignment
Pocket

Name _____

Address _____

Phone _____ Birthdate _____

Dept. _____

Class _____

Church Relationship _____

Please date and sign below:

DATE	VISITORS

116

Reach Out Prospect Assignment Card

Name _____

Address _____

Phone _____ Birthdate _____

Dept. _____

Class _____

Church Relationship _____

_____

Comments: _____

_____

DATE	REPORT OF VISIT
	Visitor:
	Visitor:
	Visitor:
	Visitor:

```
┌─────────────────┐        DEACON FAMILY INFORMATION
│                 │              Form D-33
│   Picture of    │
│  family from    │     Family_____
│    church       │
│   directory     │     Address_____
│                 │
│                 │     Telephone_____
└─────────────────┘
```

Assigned to:_____For:_____
                 Deacon's Name   Assignment Period

FAMILY MEMBERS

Name	Church Member?	Where?	Date Joined	Date of Birth

Husband's Occupation_____Business firm and

Address_____

_____Telephone _____

Wife's Occupation_____Business firm and

Address_____

_____Telephone _____

Other helpful information (special family needs, children away,
other persons in home, etc.)_____

_____

_____

_____

_____

Wedding anniversary date_____

118

RECORD OF DEACON MINISTRY

1. Date of ministry_____Type of ministry: Personal visit _____

   Letter_____Phone call _____ Other_____

   _____ Purpose of ministry _____

   _____

   Comments_____

   _____

   _____

2. Date of ministry_____Type of ministry: Personal visit_____

   Letter_____Phone call_____Other_____

   _____ Purpose of ministry_____

   _____

   Comments_____

   _____

   _____

3. Date of ministry_____Type of ministry: Personal visit_____

   Letter_____Phone call_____Other_____

   _____ Purpose of ministry_____

   _____

   Comments _____

   _____

   _____

4. Date of ministry_____Type of ministry: Personal visit_____

   Letter_____Phone call_____Other_____

   _____ Purpose of ministry_____

   _____

   Comments_____

   _____

   _____

Other Deacons Who Have Been Assigned to This Family:

Deacon_____ Date (from)_____(to)_____

Deacon_____ Date (from)_____(to)_____

New Baby Letter

Dear Friends:

We are happy to have learned that the Lord has blessed your home
with a new baby. Congratulations! I know these are days of excitement
and happiness for you. May God bless your new baby with a healthy body,
good mind, strong character, and most important of all, spiritual growth!

It is certainly a tremendous responsibility to be a parent. Not only do
you do your best to provide for your child's physical needs, but also for
moral and spiritual direction. Perhaps the best thing you can ever give
your child is a good example.

As pastor of the Tower Grove Baptist Church, I assure you our church
wants to be of service to you in any way it can. If I personally can ever
be of any help, don't hesitate to call upon me.

Again, congratulations, and God bless you and your little baby.

In Christ,

Larry Lewis, Pastor

LL:nb

Sympathy Letter

Dear   :

On behalf of the Tower Grove Baptist Church, let me express our sympathy
in the death of your   . We will be praying for you during this
difficult time. I am sure you will agree in times like this our faith is
made more dear. It is good to know the funeral is not the finish and the
grave is not the home. Jesus said, "He that believeth in Me, though he
were dead, yet shall he live: And whosoever liveth and believeth in Me
shall never die" (John 11:25-26). Let me know if there is any way I can
be of help.

In Christ,

Larry Lewis, Pastor

LL:nb

"And God shall wipe away all tears from their eyes." Revelation 7:17

120

DEACON REPORT

Date: _____

Family Visits: _____

New Member Visits: _____

Hospital Visits: _____

Fvangelistic Visits: _____

Total Visits: _____

Souls Won to Christ: _____

Comments: _____

_____

_____

_____

_____

_____

Name _____

YES—I REALLY CARE—YOU CAN COUNT ON ME
Personal Commitment Card
Church Bus Evangelism

The following is my personal commitment to our enlarged outreach in our Church Bus Evangelism:
(Please circle one or more items.)

1. Bus Captain
2. Co-captain
3. Bus Driver
4. Substitute Driver
5. Teenage Crusader
6. Bus renovation & maintenance
7. Martha Club
8. Give money ($_____) to buy buses
9. Assist in Children's Church Services
10. Any way I can.
(Explanations on other side.)

Name _____

Telephone _____ Date _____

Bus Team Responsibilities

1. BUS CAPTAIN: Leader of a team for one bus route. VISIT FOUR HOURS OR MORE EACH WEEK ENLISTING RIDERS. Make sure bus is filled each Sunday.
2. CO-CAPTAIN: Give general assistance to the Bus Captain. Help with the special activity for the bus riders one Sunday afternoon each month (picnic, party, etc.).
3. BUS DRIVER: KEEP THE BUS CLEAN, fueled, maintained, and ready to go on time each Sunday. DRIVE THE BUS SAFELY.
4. SUBSTITUTE DRIVER: Available as a substitute driver. Drive a bus usually one Sunday per month or more.
5. TEENAGE CRUSADER: Ride a bus each Sunday and assist with children (singing, etc.). Assist with Saturday visitation to enlist riders when possible.
6. BUS RENOVATION AND MAINTENANCE: Help renovate and prepare buses for painting. Assist in maintenance of buses.
7. MARTHA CLUB: Assist in preparing and serving breakfast (at 8:45) each Saturday for the bus workers.
8. GIVE MONEY TO BUY BUSES: Each bus will cost about $1,500. We need _____ buses this year and about _____ buses next year.
9. ASSIST IN CHILDREN'S CHURCH SERVICES: Assist with singing, Bible teaching, flannelgraph, etc. each Sunday morning.
10. ANY WAY I CAN: We will discuss with you the best way you can serve.

Form BE0172 CBE Supply, P.O. Box 90361, Nashville, Tn. 37209.
Copyright 1972 by Church Bus Evangelism Supply Co.

```
┌─────────────────────────────────────────────────────────────┐
│              BUS WORKER REPORT CARD                           │
│  BUS WORKER REPORT FOR SUNDAY MORNING - after bus returns     │
│  Bus #_____Captain_____Worker_____  │
│  Name _____  │
│  Time Departed_____Time Arrived_____  │
│  Profession of Faith_____By Letter_____  │
│  Attendance:  Riders_____Workers_____Total_____│
│  New Riders_____  │
│  Present on Saturday_____Yes_____No_____  │
│  Hours Visiting_____Current:_____New:_____  │
│  Person Contacted____Current:_____New:_____  │
└─────────────────────────────────────────────────────────────┘
```

124

Welcome Letter

Dear Friends:

It has been brought to my attention that you have recently moved into our area. Certainly, I join with many others in welcoming you to St. Louis. We wish you a long and happy stay in your new home.

As pastor of the Tower Grove Baptist Church, I assure you our church wants to be of service to you in any way we can. Don't hesitate to call upon me personally if I can ever be of any assistance. Day or night, I always want to be available to you if needed.

On behalf of our entire church membership, may we extend to you a cordial invitation to visit in our services? Our church is located at 4257 Magnolia Avenue, across from Missouri Botanical Gardens and Tower Grove Park, and is easily accessible by car or bus. We are only minutes away by the freeway, from nearly any area of St. Louis.

Sunday School is at 9:30 a.m. Sunday morning, and the morning worship services are at 8:15 a.m. and at 10:45 a.m. We have Church Training at 6:00 p.m. with Sunday evening worship service at 7:10 p.m. Wednesday evening worship service is at 7:30 p.m.

Tower Grove is a Bible-believing church with a Bible-centered ministry. You will find a warm welcome and a friendly atmosphere at Tower Grove.

God bless you, and welcome to our community.

Sincerely,

Larry Lewis, Pastor

LL:nb

Enclosure: Church Brochure

Acknowledgement Letter

It was a great joy to have you with us at the Tower Grove Baptist
Church. We hope you enjoyed the services and will be with us as
often as possible.

If you live in our area and are anxious to find a church home, let
me urge you to consider Tower Grove. I believe our church can be
a real blessing to your life, and I know you can be a blessing to
us. We have a full program of activities designed to give you the
best in spiritual training and Christian fellowship. This program
includes Sunday School, Church Training, Baptist Women, Brotherhood,
Royal Ambassadors, Girls in Action, Acteens, and a complete music
program. Our youth and recreation programs are considered by many
to be outstanding.

May the Lord bless you in your service to Him. If I can ever be of
any help to you, don't hesitate to let me know.

                                        In Christ,

                                        Larry Lewis, Pastor
LL:nb

Baptismal Letter

Dear Friend:

There will be a baptismal service Sunday at the beginning of each of
our worship services, for those of you who are candidates for baptism.
You need to come to my office at 8:15 a.m., 10:15 a.m., or 6:30 p.m.,
so that you will have plenty of time to prepare. Robes and towels are
furnished by the church.

Baptism is a solemn ceremony symbolizing your personal trust and
dedication to the Lord Jesus Christ. It is one of the most meaningful
experiences of your life. We are proud that you have desired to be
baptized in obedience to Christ's command, and I pray you will never
let anything discourage you in your effort to live for Him who died
for us.

                                        In Christ,

                                        Larry Lewis, Pastor
Read: Acts 2:37-38
        Acts 9:35-38
        Romans 6:3-17
        Matthew 3:3-17
        Mark 16:16

LL:nb   **126**

Membership Letter

    We want to take this opportunity to welcome you into our
church family and wish the blessings of the Lord upon your life
as we serve Him together here at Tower Grove Baptist Church.
We trust that your stay here will be a long, fruitful, and happy
one and that we will be a blessing to one another and to our
Lord.

    May I invite you to attend our New Members Class which
meets weekly, Sunday evenings at 6:00 p.m.? The class includes
four sessions designed to instruct you concerning the meaning of
church membership, the history and doctrines of Baptists, and
the nature of our church. You can begin attending the class any
Sunday. My wife and I conduct the class, which meets in the
church Fellowship Hall.

                                    In Christ,

                                    Larry Lewis, Pastor
    LL:nb

Marriage Letter

Dear Friends:

Congratulations on your recent marriage! May I wish God's blessing upon
you and your new home.

God, Himself, is the Author and Founder of the home; and I pray you will
sincerely include Him as an important Partner in your marriage. May your
home become a house of God, where the Lord is honored day by day!

As pastor of Tower Grove Baptist Church, I assure you our church wants to
be of service to you in any way it can. If I personally can ever be of any
help, don't hesitate to call upon me.

You may be interested to know that in addition to our regular worship
services at 8:15 and 10:45 a.m. and 7:10 p.m. Sundays, we have a special
Young Married Couples' Department in both Sunday School, at 9:30 a.m. and
Church Training, at 6:00 p.m.

Again, congratulations, and may God richly bless you in every way.

                                    Sincerely,

                                    Larry Lewis, Pastor
LL:nb

SELECTED BIBLIOGRAPHY

A. BOOKS

1. Anderson, Andy, *Where Action Is*. Nashville, Tennessee: Broadman Press, 1976. 158 pp.
2. Barnette, J.N., *The Pull of the People*. Nashville, Tennessee: Convention Press, 1956. 115 pp.
3. Belew, M. Wendell, *Churches and How They Grow*. Nashville, Tennessee: Broadman Press, 1971. 144 pp.
4. Bounds, E.M., *Power through Prayer*. Grand Rapids, Michigan: Zondervan Publishing House, 1962. 87 pp.
5. Burnett, Sibley C., *Better Vacation Bible Schools*. Nashville, Tennessee: Convention Press, 1957. 141 pp.
6. Dean, Kenneth M., *People Search Guide*. Nashville, Tennessee: Convention Press, 1973. 56 pp.
7. Dobbins, Gaines S., *The Churchbook*. Nashville, Tennessee: Broadman Press, 1951. 230 pp.
8. Douglas, Mack R., *How to Build an Evangelistic Church*. Grand Rapids, Michigan: Zondervan Publishing House, 1963. 88 pp.
9. Douglas Mack R., *How to Make a Habit of Succeeding*. Grand Rapids, Michigan: Zondervan Publishing House, 1966. 184 pp.
10. Edge, Findley B., *A Quest for Vitality in Religion*. Nashville, Tennessee: Broadman Press, 1963. 239 pp.
11. Edwards, Gene, *How to Have a Soul Winning Church*. Springfield, Missouri: Gospel Publishing House, 1962. 247 pp.
12. Entzminger, Louis, *How to Organize and Administer a Great Sunday School*. Fort Worth, Texas: The Manney Company, 1949. 119 pp.
13. Feather, R. Othal, *Outreach Evangelism Through the Sunday School*. Nashville, Tennessee: Convention Press, 1972. 143 pp.

14. Flake, Arthur, *Building a Standard Sunday School.* Nashville, Tennessee: Convention Press, 1922. 147 pp.
15. Foshee, Howard B., *The Ministry of the Deacon.* Nashville, Tennessee: Convention Press, 1968. 125 pp.
16. Hogue, C.B., *I Want My Church to Grow.* Nashville, Tennessee: Broadman Press, 1977. 159 pp.
17. Hyles, Jack, *How to Boost Your Church Attendance.* Grand Rapids, Michigan: Zondervan Publishing House, 1958. 99 pp.
18. Kennedy, D. James, *Evangelism Explosion.* Wheaton, Illinois: Tyndale House Publishers, 1970. 187 pp.
19. Lindsay, Dr. Homer G., Jr., *How We're Building a New Testament Church.* Decatur, Georgia: The Southern Baptist Journal, 1975. 142 pp.
20. Lovett, C.S., *Visitation Made Easy.* Baldwin Park, California: Personal Christianity, 1964. 80 pp.
21. McGavran, Donald, *Understanding Church Growth.* Grand Rapids, Michigan: William B. Eerdman's Publishing Company, 1970. 369 pp.
22. Powell, William A., *Church Bus Evangelism.* Decatur, Georgia: Woodlawn Baptist Church, 1971. 235 pp.
23. Powell, William A., *Establishing an Aggressive Bus Ministry.* Nashville, Tennessee: Church Growth Publications, 1973. 239 pp.
24. Ravenhill, Leonard, *Why Revival Tarries.* Minneapolis, Minnesota: Bethany Fellowship, 1959. 175 pp.
25. Roberson, Lee, *Double Breasted.* Murfreesboro, Tennessee: Sword of the Lord Publishers, 1977. 200 pp.
26. Scarborough, L.R., *With Christ After the Lost.* Nashville, Tennessee: Broadman Press, 1952. 286 pp.
27. Skelton, Eugene, *Ten Fastest Growing Southern Baptist Sunday Schools.* Nashville, Tennessee: Broadman Press, 1974. 152 pp.
28. Towns, Elmer, *The Ten Largest Sunday Schools.* Grand Rapids, Michigan: Baker Book House Company, 1969. 163 pp.

29. Towns, Elmer L., *America's Fastest Growing Churches.* Nashville, Tennessee: Impact Books, 1972. 218 pp.
30. Wagner, C. Peter, *Your Church Can Grow.* Glendale, California: G/L Regal Books, 1976. 171 pp.
31. Washburn, A.V., *Outreach for the Unreached.* Nashville, Tennessee: The Convention Press, 1960. 27 pp.
32. Witty, Robert G., *Church Visitation Theory and Practice.* Nashville, Tennessee: Broadman Press, 1967. 74 pp.

B. SPECIAL TYPES

33. Bright, Bill, *How to Experience and Share the Abundant Life in Christ.* San Bernadino, California: Campus Crusade for Christ International, 1968. 195 pp.
34. Cox, William R., editor, *Ideas for Training Sunday School Leaders.* Nashville, Tennessee: The Sunday School Board of the Southern Baptist Convention, 1971. 47 pp.
35. McDonough, Reginald M., compiled by, *Outreach with Church Buses.* Nashville, Tennessee: Convention Press, 1972. 50 pp.

C. PERIODICALS

36. Baptist Press Release (author unidentified), "S B C Membership Tops 13 Million," *Word and Way,* Jefferson City, Missouri: Missouri Baptist Convention, February 23, 1978.
37. Powell, William A., "The Basic Laws of Church Growth," *Southern Baptist Journal,* Buchanan, Georgia: Baptist Faith and Message Fellowship of Southern Baptists, April, 1974. p. 8
38. Towns, Elmer, "The Big Get Bigger," *Christian Life,* Wheaton, Illinois: Christian Life Publications, October 1976. p. 36
39. Towns, Elmer, "Trends in Sunday School," *Christian Life,* Wheaton, Illinois: Christian Life Publications, October, 1976. p. 37

40. _____, "The 100 Largest Sunday Schools Chart," *Christian Life,* Wheaton, Illinois: Christian Life Publications, October, 1976. p. 38

D. UNPUBLISHED MATERIALS

41. Denney, H. Joe and McElreach, Jesse D., *70 Onward, Church and Associational Phases.* Nashville, Tennessee: Baptist Sunday School Board, September, 1966. Unpublished research paper. 226 pp.
42. Lewis, Larry L., *The Bus Ministry.* Harrisburg, Pennsylvania, 1971.
43. Wagner, Peter, *The Growing Church.* Pasadena, California: Department of Church Growth, Fuller Evangelistic Association, 1975. Workbook/Study Guide with Cassette tapes. 6 Tapes.

SUPPLEMENTARY BIBLIOGRAPHY

A. BOOKS

Autrey, C.E., *Basic Evangelism.* Grand Rapids, Michigan: Zondervan Publishing House, 1959. 174 pp.

Bisagno, John R., *How to Build an Evangelistic Church.* Nashville, Tennessee: Broadman Press, 1971. 160 pp.

Barnette, J.N., *A Church Using Its Sunday School.* Nashville, Tennessee: Convention Press, 1951. 137 pp.

Coggin, James E., *You Can Reach People Now.* Nashville, Tennessee: Broadman Press, 1971. 160 pp.

Costas, Orlando E., *The Church and Its Mission: A Shattering Critique from the Third World.* Wheaton, Illinos: Tyndale House Publishers, Inc., 1974. 313 pp.

Dehoney, Wayne, *Set the Church Afire*. Nashville, Tennessee: Broadman Press, 1971. 156 pp.

Gentry, Gardiner, *Bus Them In*. Nashville, Tennessee: Church Growth Publications, 1973. 151 pp.

Green, Hollis L., *Why Churches Die*. Minneapolis, Minnesota: Bethany Fellowship, 1972. 215 pp.

Harral, Stewart, *Handbook of Effective Church Letters*. New York: Abingdon Press, 1965. 202 pp.

Harrell, W.A., *Planning Better Church Buildings*. Nashville Tennessee: Broadman Press, 1947. 182 pp.

Hyles, Jack, *Let's Build an Evangelistic Church*. Murfrees-boro, Tennessee: Sword of the Lord Publishers, 1962. 144 pp.

Matthews, C.E., *The Southern Baptist Program of Evangelism*. Nashville, Tennessee: Convention Press, 1956. 209 pp.

McBeth, Leon, *The First Baptist Church of Dallas*. Grand Rapids, Michigan: Zondervan Publishing House, 1968. 350 pp.

Morris, Charles H., *Preparation and Promotion of a Revival*. Grand Rapids, Michigan: Zondervan Publishing House, 1956. 56 pp.

B. UNPUBLISHED MATERIALS

Bonham, Tal. D., *Plan Book for a Four Day Revival*. Oklahoma City, Oklahoma: Baptist General Convention of Oklahoma. Syllabus.

Bonham, Tal. D., *Crusade Plan Book*. Oklahoma City, Oklahoma: Baptist General Convention of Oklahoma, 1975. Unpublished Handbook.